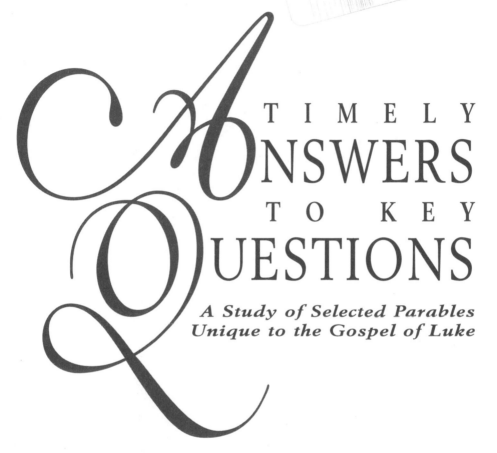

A TIMELY ANSWERS TO KEY QUESTIONS

A Study of Selected Parables
Unique to the Gospel of Luke

by Frank Pollard

Adult Winter Bible Study
Copyright 1997 ▪ Convention Press
All right reserved.

PRODUCTION TEAM

WAYNE OZMENT
Editor

CAROL DEMUMBRUM

Graphic Designer

MELISSA FINN

Technical Specialist

ANGELYN GOLMON

Production Specialist

Buelah V. Thigpen

Ross H. McLaren

Biblical Studies Specialists

Send questions/comments to:
Wayne Ozment, Editor
127 Ninth Avenue North
Nashville, TN 37234-0172

MANAGEMENT PERSONNEL

RICK EDWARDS

Manager, Adult Biblical Studies Section

LOUIS B. HANKS

Director, Biblical Studies Department

BILL L. TAYLOR
Director, Bible Teaching-Reaching Division

ISBN: 0-7673-2073-5
This book is a resource for Developing Teaching Skills course (LS-0053)
of the Leadership and Skill Development category in the subject area Biblical Studies (CG-0374)
in the Christian Growth category of the Christian Growth Study Plan.
Subject Heading: Bible. New Testament. Luke/Jesus Christ-Parables
Dewey Decimal Classification Number: 226.4
Printed in the United States of America
Bible Teaching-Reaching Division
The Sunday School Board of the Southern Baptist Convention
127 Ninth Avenue North
Nashville, Tennessee 37234

We believe the Bible has God for its author, salvation for its end, and truth, without any mixture of error for its matter. The 1963 statement of *The Baptist Faith and Message* is our doctrinal guideline. Unless otherwise stated,
Scripture quotations in this book are from the *New American Standard Bible*, copyright © The Lockman Foundation,
1960, 1962, 1963, 1968, 1971, 1973, 1975, 1977, 1995. Used by permission.

To order additional copies of this resource: WRITE Customer Service Center, 127 Ninth Avenue North, Nashville, TN
37234-0113; FAX order to (615) 251-5933; PHONE 1-800-458-2772; EMAIL to CompuServe ID 70423,2526; or visit the
Baptist Book Store serving you.

T A B L E

O F

C O N T E N T S

COVER PHOTOS BY THE STOCK MARKET

How to Become a Christian

Are You a Believer?

"I am a believer." Most likely, this statement is true of you. It accurately describes anyone who believes something. It describes you if you believe, for example, the earth is round or two plus two equals four. It also describes you if you believe the earth is flat or two plus two equals five. What you believe is not relevant to whether or not you are a believer. Even if what you believe is not true, you are still a believer.

You are a believer.

In one sense the statement "I am a believer" is true of almost everyone. All people who are capable of thinking believe something. Even those who say they don't believe anything believe they are stating the truth. So they too are believers.

You are a believer.

In another sense, however, the statement is true of relatively few people—only a minority of the world's population. It describes only those who believe in Jesus Christ. This kind of belief refers to more than what a person thinks about Jesus. It refers to those who are so certain about Jesus Christ and who He is (God) that they commit themselves to Him. Thus *believer* describes one who is a Christian.

Are you a believer?

You can become a believer in this last sense of the word by taking these simple steps:

- acknowledging that you are a sinner,
- repenting of your sin,
- asking Christ to forgive your sin, and
- committing your life to Him.

If you have done this, you are a Christian. **You are a believer.**

Several steps need to follow this conversion experience. They include joining a church and being baptized, by which you publicly acknowledge your belief in Jesus. These steps also include growing in your relationship with Jesus Christ and helping others begin and grow in their relationship with Him. Other Christians will be glad to assist you in learning how to take these further steps.

Are you a believer?

1

HOW DOES GOD FEEL ABOUT PEOPLE WHO MESS UP?

SCRIPTURE VERSES

▪Luke 15:1,11-32

A leader in the first church I served said to me, "Preacher, when you read the text from the Bible, I know what you are going to say. I have been listening to sermons for 50 years, and I always know what's coming next."

Preaching from Luke 15

As a preacher I almost cringe to announce Luke 15 as the basis for a sermon. I know that many who listen to me will say to themselves, "I know that story" or "I have heard this one all my life." If a popularity poll were taken of stories or parables told through the years, I am certain this one would rank in the top three. It is one of the most famous short stories ever voiced or written. It tells about a young man who messed up, and all of us can identify with that.

God's Word is never just an old story. It is fresh and powerful each time we read it.

Problems come from "knowing," especially if it means the person has stopped learning. For example, pity the poor Little League coach of youngsters whose parents "know" baseball.

Jesus was given the hardest time in His hometown. Why? Because the people there "knew" Him. Thinking they already knew Him, they could not know Him. The enemies of Christ knew the Scriptures best, but they criticized Him the most. Ironical, is it not? They had studied about the coming Messiah for generations. They "knew" what He would be like and what the Messiah would do when He came. Yet they did not know Him when He arrived on the scene.

The writer, teacher, or preacher who faces a well-known text has a problem. The temptation is to try to find a new or different approach, as did a preacher who announced one Sunday morning that he would preach about the prodigal son from the viewpoint of the fattened calf. I prefer, however, to approach this well-known bit of Holy Writ with reverence and awe. God's Word is never just an old story. It is fresh and powerful each time we read it.

? Application Question: ?

What facts do you already know about the parable of the prodigal son? List them: *Leave Home, Take all His money Went into the World. Spent all His money. The Come home to his father. The father Welcomed His son with a feast of a fatted Calf*

Why Did Jesus Tell the Parable?

The first question to ask about this parable is, Why and to whom did Jesus tell it? Luke 15:1-3 answers this important question. An audience of "tax-gatherers and sinners" were listening to Jesus. Because He spent time with those people who morally and spiritually had messed up, the Pharisees and scribes criticized Him. They muttered with contempt and disdain, "This man receives sinners and eats with them" (15:2). To these Pharisees and scribes—the respectable, religious people—Jesus told three parables, including the one often called the parable of the prodigal son.

Why Did Jesus Spend Time with Sinners?

We have heard all our lives, You can always tell what a person is like by the kind of company he or she keeps. Honestly now, don't you want to agree with the critical Pharisees? At first glance it looks as if they were right. Don't you tell your teenagers to stay away from sinners? What would you tell your daughter if she brought home a male "thing" with purple-spiked hair, scraggly beard, wearing pink jeans with holes in the knees? Wouldn't you feel like saying, "Watch the company you keep"?

My dad used to say, "You are who you run with." Scripture supports this saying. "In the last days difficult times will come. For men will be lovers of self, lovers of money, boastful, arrogant, revilers, disobedient to parents, ungrateful, unholy, unloving, irreconcilable, malicious gossips, without self-control, brutal, haters of good, treacherous, reckless, conceited, lovers of pleasure rather than lovers of God; holding to a form of godliness, although they have denied its power; and *avoid such men as these*" (2 Tim. 3:1-5; italics added).

You cannot always accurately describe people by the company they keep. Would you say doctors are sick because they spend time with sick people, or funeral directors are dead because they are constantly in the presence of the deceased, or kindergarten teachers are ignorant because they spend hours with people who cannot read? Neither can you say Christ was sinful because He spent time with sinful people.

Jesus spent time with people most others were careful to avoid because He loved people. He always distinguished between the sinner and the sin.

Why Did Sinners Spend Time with Jesus?

A better question than Why did Jesus spend time with sinners? is Why did sinners spend time with Jesus? Some may say that Jesus' wanting to be with sinners is amazing, but I think their wanting to be with Him is even more amazing.

Have you noticed in the biblical accounts that Jesus' goodness was never offensive? The worst people felt at ease with Him. He was perfect. He never sinned, yet sinners were happy to be with Him. His goodness never offended them. Amazing!

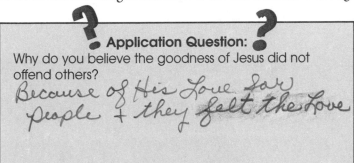

Application Question:
Why do you believe the goodness of Jesus did not offend others?

Because of His Love for people + they felt the Love

Jesus accepted all people. He loved all people. He spent time with all kinds of people, listened to their stories, and told a few of His own. They loved Him because He loved them.

How Did Jesus Respond to His Critics?

The critical religious leaders leveled their judgment at Jesus by citing the company He kept. He responded by telling three parables related to one theme. A sheep wandered off, got lost, was sought, and was joyously found. A coin was misplaced carelessly and was recovered with great joy. A son broke his father's heart by demanding his due and then taking off to far places. When he returned, his father held a joyful celebration. These parables clearly show that God loves and responds positively to those who have messed up their lives; when they come to Him, He welcomes them. No matter where you are, the Heavenly Father is anxious to have you where you belong. He wants you to know that your place in His mansion is ready and waiting.

Application Question:
Can you think of a time in your life when you "messed up" and God showed He loved you? Write a brief prayer of thanks to God for His love and grace. *Dear Father I thank you for picking me up & lots of times you have carried me. I through all the times I've messed up. I give you all the Glory & Praise In Jesus name a-men*

Looking for What You've Got

We mess up when we go looking in strange places for what we already have. Jesus made this point clear in the last of these three parables. A young man left home one day searching for something and came home another day to find it (15:11-16).

Something like that happens to people all the time. They look in strange places, do strange things, and then they come back home to find what they were seeking.

Application Question:
What are some of the things that people you know "leave home searching for" today? *Relationships Peace of mind money Happiness*

PRAYER LIST
January 11, 1998

Kenny Marcum	Mr. & Mrs. Dixon	Everett Clemmons	Jeremy Greenup
Cecil & Laura Loyall	Paul Meredith	Barbara Etherton	Grace Townsend
Mrs. Spratt/Family	Lost	Pauline Ash	Coy Sanders
Elsie Keplinger	Sandy Helm	Norman Douglas	Gia/Branti
Debbie Knox Family	Mrs. Daugherty	Dory Bryant	Beaver's Half Sister
Bruce Hart	Mitchell Hunt	Ruth Ann Jones	Logan McFelia
Rita Cruse	Jail Ministry	Mr. Mosley (Ala)	Stella Crain
Youth/Associate Pastor	Harold Ray	James Revo	Carolina Rice (Bush)
Rachel Willoughby	Unspoken	Margaret Keith	Ruby Ford
Linda Pyzocha	Lloyd Littleton	Jinny Shaw	Pat Langley
Mr. Boone	William J. Bryan	Boola Cromer	Jim Fields
Mable Cable	Dean Duncan Family		

PRAYER NEEDS OF VALLEY CREEK BAPTIST CHURCH FOR 1998

1. Pray that all layman and laywomen will step forward and allow God to use them in His ministry and work.

2. Pray for the Associate Pastor Search Committee. Pray that God will show us the man that fits the qualifications of Associate Pastor at Valley Creek.

3. Pray for the Minister of Youth Search Committee. Pray that God will show us the man that fits the qualifications for Minister of Youth at Valley Creek.

4. Pray for the reduction and eventual retirement of Valley Creek's building debt. Pray for the Building Committee as they move forward to finalize plans for an Educational Wing - A wing which would be used to further Bible Study and Prayer Ministries.

5. Pray for Valley Creek's Sunday School. Pray that all people in our congregation would become involved in the study of God's word each Sunday morning.

6. Pray that an organized Prayer Ministry will be started and that it will have many volunteers to keep it going.

7. Pray for Bro. Steve in his ministry as pastor of Valley Creek. Pray each week for him as he prepares his sermons and as he ministers to our church family and our community.

8. Pray for our children's classes and our youth and the many dedicated people who work with them each week.

9. Pray for our special classes that meet each week or month. Classes such as the Ladies' Bible Study Group, Strugglers, P.Y.P., Winter Bible Study, First Place, Men's Prayer Breakfast, U.C.T., Youth Celebration - ¿ LIFE ?, etc.

10. Pray for our Van Ministry. Pray that we will continue to have dedicated people who are willing to work with this ministry, and that we will have more people who will volunteer to help.

11. Pray for our Kentucky Ministry for Crime Prevention. Pray that lives will be changed because of our church's willingness to reach out to troubled youth in our community.

In this parable we see the whole process of searching, doing, and then returning. The process is born of a yearning to experience life in its fullness. This yearning leads each of us at one time or another in varying degrees to say, "Give me my due."

Most of life's biggest disappointments come from wanting something bigger than we are getting. Who of us is not aware that we are made for something higher than we are reaching? Yet this hunger often prompts people not to reach up but to stoop down.

That is what happened to this young man. In city after city, sensation after sensation, he sought life and never found it. The more he looked, the less he lived. The more he did what he liked, the less he liked what he did. The more he fed the hunger, the closer he came to famine.

How to Find Yourself

This young man had set out for Utopia and ended up in a pig's pen. The Bible says, "He came to his senses" (15:17). The *King James Version* reads, "He came to himself." He had not been himself since he left home. When he came to his senses, he realized he had only emptiness and guilt left. This young man provides us a pattern for turning around and coming to the Father. How do we find ourselves and enter into a proper relationship with our Heavenly Father?

First, you have to honestly face yourself. No longer could the younger son escape life's harshest truth in glaring lights or blaring sounds. When he faced himself, he did not like what he saw. What he said in 15:17-18 could be paraphrased as, *What is the son of my father doing here? I will go back home and tell him that I have sinned.*

Some say our whole nation is caught up in a guilt complex. While some people feel guilty when they should not, most of us feel guilty because we are guilty. Forgiveness and peace of mind can be found only in the Father's presence, and we take the first step toward Him by admitting our sinfulness.

Too often I have heard others make light of God's people by saying, "I am no hypocrite. I do not go to church and pretend I am something I am not." Exactly the opposite is true. We who are in God's kingdom do not pretend to be what we are not. We have admitted we are sinners. We know we are not perfect. We do not go to church to play a part; we go because we know our weakness. We know we need God's grace and forgiveness. Also, we need the fellowship and acceptance of other sinners who have been saved by the grace of God. The real hypocrites are those who know they need Almighty God's saving grace and pretend they do not. The first step toward finding yourself is facing yourself.

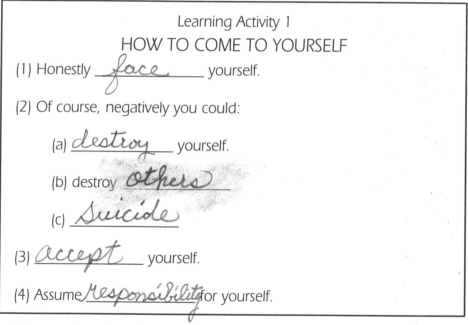

Learning Activity 1

HOW TO COME TO YOURSELF

(1) Honestly __*face*__ yourself.

(2) Of course, negatively you could:

(a) __*destroy*__ yourself.

(b) destroy __*others*__

(c) __*Suicide*__

(3) __*accept*__ yourself.

(4) Assume __*responsibility*__ for yourself.

When you have faced up to the guilt in your life, what then? What can you do? Well, you can do several things, not all of which are healthy.

You could destroy yourself. Judas did. He said, "I have sinned by betraying innocent blood" (Matt. 27:4). He could not handle what he did, so he went out and took his life. Suicide is not the only way to destroy yourself. Some do it gradually with alcohol or other narcotics; or they spend their waking hours belittling themselves, punishing themselves in various creative ways.

If you do not handle your guilt by destroying yourself, you could decide to destroy others. You may say to yourself, "I may be guilty, but then so is everyone else." So you make your life's goal to search out and to expose the wrong in others. If you cannot find it, you assume it. The gossiper is nothing more than a small person who wants to make sure everyone else is just as small.

Another way of handling guilt is to quit. Just drop out. You do not want to destroy yourself, and you do not want to destroy others. Neither do you want to change yourself or to help others. So you just quit.

The next step toward finding yourself and God is none of these; rather it is to accept yourself. You can take a good honest look at yourself and say, "This is what I am. These are my limitations, but I can start right here." At one time or another we all have to face up to ourselves, accept what we are, and then move on.

After you face yourself and accept yourself, then you need to assume responsibility for yourself. Every now and then I hear someone say, "I have not been to church in months, and no one missed me," or "I was in the hospital for days, and no one came to see me." Such a person is saying, "The church is responsible for me, and the church did not come through." To a degree, this is true; and I would never want the church to dodge that responsibility. Is it not also true that each church member is responsible too? I always feel like saying, "Yes, we are responsible for you; but you are responsible too."

Today's favorite indoor-outdoor sport may well be dodging responsibility.

The prodigal son realized that he was responsible for himself. His life would never have changed if he had not faced that fact. Today's favorite indoor-outdoor sport may well be dodging responsibility. The son could have said, "This is my father's fault. He should not have given me that money. He should have made me stay home." The son could have sat in the mud, patting a pig and waiting for something to happen. Instead he choose another path. Listen to the responsibility in his statement, "I will get up and go to my father, and will say to him, 'Father, I have sinned.'" Just because he left did not mean he had to stay away.

I am told good businessmen have an inventory indicating the location of all the tools, all the equipment, and all the material they own. What a strange commentary on our lives—we know how to find things, but we have a most difficult time finding ourselves.

Application Question:

In what positions and possessions have you been tempted to find your identity? Write them here:

A boy once was having a hard time remembering where he had left things. He decided to write himself a note just before he went to sleep, "Your shoes are under the bed; your clothes are on the chair; your cap is hanging in the closet; your money, your knife, and your baseball cards are on the bureau; and you are in the bed." In the morning he found everything precisely as the note indicated, with one exception. When he looked in the bed, he was not there; he could not find himself. That is not the story of the prodigal.

The prodigal came to himself when there was nothing left but himself (15:18-19). I once read about an epitaph that tacks a terrible truth on the wall of our aware-

What a strange commentary on our lives— we know how to find things, but we have a most difficult time finding ourselves.

ness, "Born a human being; Died a wholesale grocer." I do not mean this as a dig aimed at grocers. This kind of remark could be made of most of us who have a high regard for our occupations. Failing to find identity in ourselves, we seek it in possessions or position, neither of which is necessarily evil. Yet what a sad commentary on eternal souls made in God's image. We have lost ourselves. We express our identity in what we have or what we do—instead of who we are.

Jesus dressed this great truth in common clothing when he presented this question, "For what does it profit a man to gain the whole world, and forfeit his

soul?" (Mark 8:36). The word translated "soul" means life, self, or yourself. So Jesus was in essence declaring, *You who are always thinking in terms of profit and loss need to listen. Let's take this all the way to the extreme. If you could obtain everything—all that's in, on, above, and under the earth—but in doing so would lose yourself, then you would suffer a titanic loss.*

Many times I have heard folk laugh at faith's simple words, *lost* and *found*. These words hold powerful truths. Do they

> The Word of God is a guide, not for finding things, but for finding yourself.

speak to you? In your heart do you know somewhere you have lost yourself? God's Word tells you how that happened and how to find yourself again. The Word of God is a guide, not for finding things, but for finding yourself.

The prodigal son found himself by going back to where he lost himself. To find yourself, you must first know where you lost yourself.

Do Not Miss Your Party

This parable has three main characters, a father and two sons. I believe, however, it is mostly about the father—a father who loved, waited for, and welcomed his prodigal son—not to a guilt trip but to a party (15:20-24).

Do you think coming to God means He will greet you saying, "You lousy, no good prodigal! I am going to make your

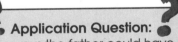

Application Question:
What are some ways the father could have responded to his younger son? *Turned in away*

life miserable"? No, a thousand times, no! He appeals to each of us, "My child, I love you. Do not miss your party." When we come home to Him, He greets us with love and dignity.

If you had been the father and your son had squandered a third of your resources in ways totally repugnant to you and he came home begging for a job, how would you have responded? Would you have said, "Well, get over to the workers' quarters, find a bunk, and we will see how it works out. And by the way, clean up and get a hair cut"? You can think of many ways the father could have reacted, but he responded with love and with concern for his son's dignity.

The father saw the son coming from a long way off because he was looking for him. He ran to his son and hugged him and kissed him. In fact, the Bible word for "kissed" means that he did so again and again and again.

You may want to say, "But preacher, you said he welcomed the son with love and dignity. All this running and hugging and kissing doesn't sound dignified to me."

When I said the father welcomed the son with love and dignity, I had in mind the father's love for his son and his concern for the son's dignity. Likewise when God welcomes us, He shows His love for us and His concern for our dignity. This young man had thoroughly rehearsed his speech. He meant it. It was proper and it was true. He had planned to say, "Father, I have sinned against heaven, and in your sight; I am no longer worthy to be called your son; make me as one of your hired men" (15:18-19). The father, however, interrupted that soliloquy of self-loathing and said, "Quickly bring out the best robe and put it on him, and put a ring on his hand and sandals on his feet" (15:22), a mark of sonship and the seal of authority. He was a free man.

The prodigal's father would not let the son dwell on his mistakes. He refused to listen to that; he had a party to arrange. The father essentially said, *The most*

Application Questions:

What is something you have turned from (repented of)?

Consider the same situation. What did you turn to?

important fact is that you are alive! You are back! Let us celebrate! When we come to our Heavenly Father, He welcomes us with love and with concern for our dignity. We come home to a party—not a guilt trip.

Please understand this: *repentance* is a positive word. It does mean to turn around. It does mean to turn your back on something, but what you turn from is not as significant as what you turn to. Repentance is not only turning *away* from something; it is turning *to* something. It is turning away from sin and turning to God.

What words do you connect with God's call to repent? Guilt? Remorse? Regret? Listen! Godly sorrow "produces a repentance without regret, leading to salvation" (2 Cor. 7:10). What a happy day when you decide you want to stop heading in hell's direction and start moving toward heaven!

Joy is in the background of the biblical call to repent. Jesus said, "Repent, for the kingdom of heaven is at hand" (Matt. 4:17). He did not say, *Repent, or hell will have you.* He could have said that because it is true, but instead He spotlighted the relationship of repentance and the kingdom. In the two parables that precede this one (Luke 15:4-10), Jesus also highlighted the direct relationship of repentance and joy. He declared there is rejoicing in heaven when one sinner repents (15:7,10).

Messing Up Without Moving Out

Have you ever wanted to edit the Bible? If so, this might be one of the places you'd choose to edit. Most people would like to end this account with the prodigal's return. Verse 24 is a happy ending, a climax, "And they began to be merry."

Hollywood certainly would let the credits roll here. The boy is back; there is a joyous homecoming; the best calf has been butchered. The smell of barbecued beef and the sound of happy music are everywhere. A huge party is in process. Turn the house lights on.

Our Lord did not end His parable there. The plot was just heating up. Jesus was getting to His main point. When His first-century critics heard Jesus mention the other prodigal,

YOUR
NOTES

(LUKE 15:1,11-32)

Application Question:
Can you think of a time when you left the Father without ever stepping off the porch? Describe that time here:

the older brother, they knew He had turned their words back at themselves (15:25-27). In essence He was saying to them, *You criticized Me for being with sinners, for helping them find their way to the Father. I have a word for you—a word you desperately need to hear.*

Jesus' critics understood His point. They were like the elder son, the one who stayed in the father's house, worked on the father's farm, performed what he perceived to be the necessary duties, yet strayed a long way from duplicating what was in his father's heart and from showing the kind of love his father showed. Many of us need to get this point too.

The Whining Christian

When the older brother came from the fields, he saw all the preparations being made and he heard the people's glad shouts. Stopping a busy servant, he asked what was going on. The servant said that his brother was back home safe and sound and his father had killed the pen-fed calf for a party. What great news! Yet the older brother was angry and would not go to the party. His father came out and pleaded with him to join in welcoming his brother. He rejected his father's invitation and complained that, though he had been faithful to his father, he had not been treated as well as his rebellious younger brother (15:28-30).

This son had left his father without stepping off the front porch. As we look at the pouting lips of the brother who pouted because he had never had a party, we see a perfect illustration of one of the most pitiful pictures in all the showcase of misunderstood faith—the whining Christian.

The Curse of Self-Pity

One tends to feel sorry for people in this situation, for they suffer from the curse of self-pity—a curse that robs and destroys. Self-pity destroys our happiness. This brother was sullen and sulky in his anger. Our life with Christ is to be a happy journey. The summons to rejoice is sounded numerous times in the New Testament. In a testimony I once heard someone say, "My cup runneth over and my saucer too." Joy is a sign of spiritual maturity. It is the outcome of the direct presence of Christ within us—a sense of well-being in Him and a sense of adequacy to meet anything that comes from without. How quickly we can kill that joy by nourishing a grievance!

Self-pity also can destroy our usefulness. The older brother was angry and would not go in to the party. How much was to be done in the household that day! The whole place teemed with activity and everyone enjoyed the work. Servants hurried here and there. The father, with a smile on his face, moved con-

tentedly among all the guests, delighted in the busy activity. Only one person—the elder brother—did nothing that day except sulk and scowl and pout.

The curse of self-pity also can destroy our oneness, our fellowship. He was angry and the Scripture says he "was not willing to go in" (15:28). The elder brother revealed a deep break in fellowship with his father when he said "this son of yours" (15:30) rather than *this brother of mine.* Thus he would not go in. Not wanting to be with your brothers and sisters is a symptom of critical, spiritual illness.

The older brother's self-pity restricted his vision. Note the repetition of the personal pronouns in his statement to his father in 15:29-30, "Look! For so many years I have been serving you, and I have never neglected a command of yours; and yet you have never given me a kid [a goat] that I might be merry with my friends; but when this son of yours came, who has devoured your wealth with harlots, you killed the fattened calf for him" (15:29-30). "I," "me," and "my" occur repeatedly. This man was suffering from "I" disease. When your vision is filled with yourself, you have restricted your vision.

Worst of all, focusing on self distorts one's values. The elder son was callous about his father's broken heart. He knew the pain his father was feeling because his younger son was lost, but he did nothing about it. He knew that his brother was lost and that his father wanted more than anything else in the world for this son to be found. The elder brother showed no concern about that. Instead he devoted himself to the tasks on the farm that one day would be his.

You Can Come Back
The beauty of this parable is that it shows both kinds of children can come home (15:31-32). The father was as patient

Application Question:
What significant decisions have you made in the last year that are directly responsible for where you are today? Consider this in terms of physical and spiritual well-being.

and compassionate toward his elder son as toward his younger son. People are special among all the creation of God. Of all He created, He allows only us human beings to determine our own destinies. God gives us the dignity and the danger of decision. We are the sum of decisions we have made: *I will go here; I will not go there. I will do this; I will not do that. I will think this; I will not think that.* Our decisions have made us who we are.

You never see anyone pat a puppy on the head and say, "Well, little doggie, what are you going to be when you grow up?" He is going to be a dog! Boys and

---

Learning Activity 2

THE IMPACT OF SELF-PITY ON THE CHURCH

Directions: As the teacher refers to each of the following, consider specific examples of ways these destructive behaviors may be expressed within churches today. List your responses in the space provided and be prepared to participate in a group discussion.

(1) Self-pity Destroys Happiness.

(2) Self-pity Destroys Usefulness.

(3) Self-pity Destroys Fellowship.

(4) Self-pity Restricts Vision.

(5) Self-pity Distorts Values.

girls grow up to be a number of different things because they can make decisions.

Of course, the greatest, most important decision of all is what to do about the Person and claims of Christ. This parable shows that God has allowed us the awesome freedom to determine our own eternal destiny.

Those who mess up by running far from God and those who mess up without moving out both can experience God's love, peace, and grace by exercising the awesome responsibility of decision. The Father loves you. He will not force His will on you. So the scriptural invitation is always an appeal for you to be responsible for your actions, a call for you to decide to come to the Father in repentance and faith.

Jesus calls to us, "Come to Me, all who are weary and heavy-laden, and I will give you rest" (Matt. 11:28). The rest for your weary life is there, but only if you come to Him. "If we confess our sins, He is faithful and righteous to forgive us our sins and to cleanse us from all unrighteousness" (1 John 1:9). The offer of total and complete forgiveness is extended. Forgiveness is yours, but only if you come to Him in repentance and faith.

God's invitation to all—prodigal sons and older brothers alike—is this: Do not miss the party!

God's invitation to all—prodigal sons and older brothers alike—is this: Do not miss the party!

C H A P T E R

2

WHAT'S SO URGENT ABOUT SALVATION?

SCRIPTURE VERSES

■Luke 14:1,15-24; 16:19-31

A t first reading, the setting of the parable about the great banquet appears to present a rather simple scene. Our Lord was sitting with others at a banquet, telling a story—just a gathering of people, important people to be sure, being taught by the Master Teacher, a somewhat casual discussion over dinner.

Not so! This was not a festive occasion.

Background Music

If we could have some background music to go along with this account, we would readily understand the situation. Music is a big part of telling the story in movies. For instance, a man is walking down a street. He is about to collide with a beautiful lady at the corner of a building. She will be knocked off her feet by the impact. Everything she is carrying, a considerable load, will be spread across the sidewalk. It happens! As the two of them are picking up the articles, their eyes meet and they fall in love. In another movie, a man is walking down a street and a sinister figure comes from the darkness of an alley and stabs him.

In each case we are set up for the action by the background music. As the first man walks down the street, the music relays the message that he is going to run into this lady; but she will not be hurt, and they will fall in love. As the second man walks down the street, we hear music that is much different from that of the first movie. This music tells us something bad is about to happen to him.

Students of the Bible have to listen to the "background music" of a passage. In it they find the mood and the tension of a scriptural episode. The Word commands, "Be diligent to present yourself approved to God as a workman who does not need to be ashamed, handling accurately the word of truth" (2 Tim. 2:15). Part of what that means is to read the Bible prayerfully, carefully, and thoroughly. Move into the text and stay until you are at home with it. Then you will hear the background music; you will understand the mood.

When you listen for the music behind this banquet scene, you hear sinister, angry, and hostile notes.

Straight Talk (Luke 14:1,15-24)

The scene took place in the home of a leading Pharisee. Other important people were there. Why did this prominent Pharisee invite Jesus to his home? What was the purpose of this gathering of religious big shots? It was more than a casual after-church gathering. "They were watching Him closely" (Luke 14:1). With narrow, judgmental, focused eyes, the Pharisees observed Him that day, making their judgments about Him.

After this day a series of meetings may have begun that led to the crucifixion of Jesus. One such meeting is recorded in Matthew 26:3-4, "Then the chief priest and elders of the people were gathered together in the court of the high priest, named Caiaphas; and they plotted together to seize Jesus by stealth, and kill Him."

Luke 14:2-14 shows that the people present at this banquet liked nothing Jesus did or said. He chided the Pharisees because they endorsed helping a son or even an ox out of a well on the Sabbath but objected to healing a person on the Sabbath. Jesus spoke critically of the guests at the meeting because they jockeyed for places of honor. He criticized the host for inviting only people who could repay his hospitality. He said, "When you give a luncheon or a dinner, do not invite your friends or your brothers or your relatives or rich neigh-

YOUR
NOTES
(LUKE 14:1,15-24)

bors, lest they also invite you in return, and repayment come to you. When you give a reception, invite the poor, the crippled, the lame, the blind, and you will be blessed, since they do not have the means to repay you; for you will be repaid at the resurrection of the righteous" (Luke 14:12-14).

Learning Activity 1
LUKE 14:1-14

Read Luke 14:1-14 to discover the background music for this story. Make notes in the space provided about possible emotions present.

Luke 14:1 *Went into the house of the Chief Pharisees to eat bread.*

Luke 14:2-3 *He spoke to the lawyers & Pharisees, Is it lawful to heal on the Sabbath day*

Luke 14:4

Luke 14:5-6

Luke 14:7-11

Luke 14:12-14

By this point Jesus had confronted and challenged almost everyone there. Can you hear the angry background music? All the people were offended.

A man at Jesus' table decided it was time to stop the discussion. He said to Jesus so all could hear, "Blessed is everyone who shall eat bread in the kingdom of God!" (14:15). Today the man's statement would be understood as meaning something like "Well, we are all going to the same place" or "All roads lead to heaven" or "It doesn't make any difference what you believe just so long as you're sincere." It was a moderating, let's-stop-the-discussion statement.

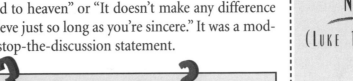

Application Question:

What do Christians say or do (not say or not do) that communicates to others "all roads lead to heaven"?

This man or one of his relatives attends every party. When the tension rises, they always say something like "Let's not be radical about this."

Application Question:

What do churches say or do (not say or not do) that communicates to the community that "all roads lead to heaven"?

Jesus pressed on. He told another parable that in essence said, *Do you not know? You will eat bread in the kingdom of heaven only if you repent and accept My invitation. If you refuse, you will not eat the feast of the kingdom of heaven.*

Why did Jesus do that? He already had angered everyone in the place. Then He told a parable that made the atmosphere even more tense. Jesus was the invited guest in another's home, and He spoke in a strong, straightforward manner. He willingly ran the risk of being considered rude. Why?

Some people like to play cutting word games. Apparently Winston Churchill did. At a gathering one evening, he and Lady Astor were trading verbal barbs; and finally, exasperated, she said, "'Mr. Churchill, if I were your wife I'd put poison in your tea.' Churchill said, 'Madame, if I were your husband, I'd drink it!'"[1]

Your Notes (Luke 14:1, 15-24)

Churchill and Bernard Shaw, the great English playwright, enjoyed trading word barbs. Mr. Shaw sent Mr. Churchill two tickets to the opening night of one of his plays. The accompanying note read, "These are two tickets for opening night of my new play, one for you and one for a friend, if you have one." Churchill sent the tickets back with the message, "I cannot attend the opening night. Send two tickets for the next night, if there is one."[2]

Application Questions:
What word games do Christians play when they have an opportunity to talk to a person about salvation? Which, if any, of these games have you ever played?

Did Jesus enjoy word fights? Did He delight in verbal jousting and throwing sharp word spears at others? Did He like to argue? Not at all! Jesus never played trivial word games. He declared, "I say to you, that every careless word that men shall speak, they shall render account for it in the day of judgment. For by your words you shall be justified, and by your words you shall be condemned" (Matt. 12:36-37). Then why this persistence? Why these hard words? He used this method to get the attention of His audience. He was in the company of people who mistakenly believed they had a lock on the kingdom of God. They were certain that if anyone was going to heaven, they were. Jesus was spurred by the urgency of sharing with these people God's way of salvation.

These words of our Lord were strong like a bolt of lightening. Mark Twain said, "Thunder is impressive; but it is lightning that does the work."[3] Jesus was warning, _You need to hear me. That's the only way you can know how to enter the kingdom._ He spoke these strong, harsh-sounding words in love. Jesus issued a compassionate warning to people who soon would engineer His demise. Ironically, Jesus' death was an act of love for the very people who opposed Him.

The Kingdom of God

The kingdom of God was the central teaching of Jesus Christ. (The term "kingdom of heaven," found in the Gospel of Matthew, carries the same meaning.) Jesus' first message was about the kingdom of God. After a time of temptation, He began His public ministry. "From that time Jesus began to preach and say, 'Repent, for the kingdom of heaven is a hand'" (Matt. 4:17). Mark 1:14-15 summarizes Jesus' preaching. The kingdom of God is the heart of that summary.

Jesus sent the disciples on a mission "to proclaim the kingdom of God, and to perform healing" (Luke 9:2). When He sent out the 70, He instructed them concerning what they were to do and to say. He told them their message was, "The kingdom of God has come near to you" (Luke 10:9).

Acts 1:3 provides this summary of Jesus' post-resurrection appearances, "He also presented Himself alive . . . speaking of the things concerning the kingdom of God."

In His ministry Jesus focused on the kingdom of God. He did that by showing the true nature of God, forgiving sins, and demonstrating the most powerful moral force in the universe, which is love. Jesus broke the power of evil. The crucified, resurrected Lord lives in His followers through the Holy Spirit. These great facts explain the breaking of evil's power.

Jesus responded to the well-meaning man's comment in 14:15 with the parable of the great supper. This parable in essence said that this man knew very little about the kingdom, what the kingdom is, who is in the kingdom, or how to enter it! To Jesus the kingdom of God is serious business, not empty Sunday talk. Jesus grasped clearly the urgency of salvation.

What Is the Kingdom of God?

This parable is about people on earth and the kingdom of God. Jesus taught us what the kingdom of God is when He taught us to pray, "Thy kingdom come. Thy will be done, On earth as it is in heaven" (Matt. 6:10). The kingdom of God is God's will being done on earth as it is in heaven. It is the reign of God in every part of life.

Application Question:
From your previous study of the Bible, what are some of the ways Jesus completed the sentence, "The kingdom of heaven (of God) is like . . ."?

Pictures of the Kingdom

Our Lord presented a variety of word pictures in describing the kingdom of God. Often He prefaced His parables with the phrase "The kingdom heaven [of God] is like . . . ." He said the kingdom is like a mustard seed (Matt. 13:31) and like leaven (Matt. 13:33). Jesus also said the kingdom is like the owner of a large estate who went away leaving all his holdings in the care of his servants. Then suddenly and unexpectedly he came back and asked for an accounting (Matt. 25:14-30). On other occasions Jesus spoke about the kingdom of God as a party, one that included a banquet. We can understand why Jesus used such a reference. Many who heard Him speak never had all they wanted to eat. What better picture of eternal joy could He give to them than that of a banquet!

Invitation to the Party

The word was sent out to "Come" (14:17). Christ's invitation is addressed to everyone. His invitation is clear and compelling and simple. There's not a word about *do this and then you can come*; not even a warning to *clean up your act and then you can come*. We are extended a just-as-we-are invitation. "Come."

Application Questions:
What are some of the stipulations that churches unintentionally place on people they invite to the kingdom of God? Which, if any, of these stipulations has your church ever used?

"Everything is ready now," stated the invitation. This is no potluck supper to which Christ invites us. You and I are not required to bring anything but ourselves to the Lord's kingdom feast. Indeed, we have nothing to bring but ourselves. We cannot achieve the kingdom; we cannot build it. The kingdom is complete. Only the absent invitee is missing.

Now is the only moment any of us are guaranteed. Salvation "is ready *now.*"

Jesus' invitation contains a note of urgency. "Everything is ready *now.*" He urges us to come now. His call is consistently in the urgent present tense. Eternal destiny is at stake. Now is the only moment any of us are guaranteed. Salvation "is ready *now.*"

What a deal! Who can refuse an offer like this? Eternal life —freely, lovingly given—is put before us for the taking.

Lame Excuses

So all those in Jesus' parable accepted the man's invitation to the banquet, right? Wrong! "They all alike began to make excuses" (14:18). Three excuses are given. The first two concerned business that was engrossing. Land had to be inspected. Newly purchased oxen needed to be tested. The third concerned a new marriage that needed attention.

The business excuses apparently were given politely. At least they each ended with a phrase that included "please." For whatever reason, however, the newly married man bluntly replied, "I have married a wife, and for that reason I cannot come" (14:20).

What do you think these same people, if invited to another banquet a year later, would have said? Doubtless business would have become more demanding. More acres and more livestock would have been purchased. Family life would have become more engrossing. Perhaps a new baby would have been born.

Were those good excuses? Before you answer, consider this old story. A farmer asked his neighbor whether he could borrow a rope.

What's your excuse?

CORELPHOTO

"Sorry, I can't let you have the rope," said the neighbor. "I use it to tie up milk."

"That's ridiculous," declared the farmer. "You can't tie up milk with a rope."

"True," the neighbor replied, "but when you don't want to do a thing, one excuse is as good as another."

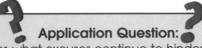

Application Question:
If you are a believer, what excuses continue to hinder your discipleship?

Excuses reveal priorities. Life boils down to priorities and choices. Our available time does not allow us freedom to do everything—even the good things we want to do. First attention is to be given to first priorities. Sometimes our excuses reveal that we give first-rate loyalties to third-rate causes. Jesus declared His kingdom must be given first priority. "Seek first His kingdom and His righteousness; and all these things shall be added to you" (Matt. 6:33).

Strange People at the Party

Note one key element in this parable depicting the kingdom as a banquet. The people who finally attended the party seemed out of place. They did not "belong." These were not the people you would expect to attend such a party.

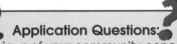

Application Questions:
Consider the popular views of your community concerning religion. What types of people would they say belong at God's banquet table?

What types of people would they say do not belong at God's banquet table?

A young minister in Minnesota observed the hurt feelings and depression of high school students without dates on Senior Prom night. John Carlson decided to do something for those not in the popular-and-beautiful crowd. He planned an alternate party for all those without dates on prom night. This prom took place on the same night as the Senior Prom, and the students loved it.

There was no stopping this party. It grew. The press heard about the second prom and spread the story. A large corporation decided to give watches to those

who attended. Other companies joined in. Soon a bag full of gifts was to be given to everyone at the alternate prom. Some students who could get dates for the Senior Prom didn't attend it. Instead they went to the other party because it was better.

BSSB PHOTO

Where are the "right" people?

The kingdom of God is the only party in eternity. Why then are the "best people" not there (Luke 18:24)? Why did Jesus say, "Truly I say to you, it is hard for a rich man to enter the kingdom of heaven" (Matt. 19:23)? Why did Paul remind the Corinthians that among them "there were not many wise according to the flesh, not many mighty, not many noble" (1 Cor. 1:26)?

You would think people would stand in line to accept the gift of salvation. People will stand in line for hours to pay big bucks for tickets to an event that will not last as long as they stood in line. Why don't they stand in line to take the gift of the best kind of life that never ends?

Why are wise, mighty, and noble people attracted to an object in reverse ratio to its worth? The more valuable something is, the less they care to have it. These people, like us all, are invited to "come; for everything is ready now." Yet they spend their efforts to get things they cannot keep and ignore the free offer of eternal riches they cannot lose.

Only people who will humble themselves and come to Christ with childlike faith will know His eternal life.

Many people turn down or ignore Jesus' invitation to eternal life because of pride. They simply cannot or will not accept God's grace. Only people who will humble themselves and come to Christ with childlike faith will know His eternal life.

Our Lord caused quite a disturbance at the banquet that day. He was aggressive, earnest, intense, and urgent in His plea. He did not want anyone there to miss what He alone could give them: salvation. He was saying to them, *Do not let your pride keep you from My party.*

To each of us today Jesus issues the same urgent invitation that the man in His parable issued, "Come, for everything is ready now."

Which Life After Death? (Luke 16:19-31)[4]

In another passage Jesus expressed the urgency of salvation even more vividly than in the parable of the great supper. He told about a rich man and a beggar named Lazarus.

A man habitually read the obituaries first thing each morning. If his name was not included, he dressed and went to work. One morning he read the obituaries and discovered his name there. Of course he was shaken, but he decided to go to work anyway.

Once at work, he called a friend and asked, "Did you read my name in the obituaries this morning?"

"Yes," said his friend. "Where are you calling from?"

The question is, If *you* should die before *you* wake, where will the Lord *your* soul take?

I want to draw for you a very tight boundary around this subject. I am not talking about someday when the Lord returns to judge the world. Even though that event could take place before you read another line, I want you to consider an immediate scenario. What would happen if you ceased breathing right now? Is there any word from God for those who go to their graves before the return of Christ and the resurrection?

The answer of course is yes. Several places in the Bible we find small windows that give some light on what we can expect immediately at death. The New Testament teaches that at death the body returns to earth and the spirit enters into a state of living existence, consisting of either blessedness or suffering. The

Word of God also affirms that at the return of Christ all bodies will be resurrected and transformed.

While we tend to divide people into many categories, you already know that God's Word has only two major groups. They are described in terms like these:

saved	or	lost
alive in Christ	or	dead in sins
children of light	or	children of darkness.

Luke 16:19-31 includes a detailed description of representatives from both groups and their destinies at death. No conjured tale is this. Our Lord did not describe this episode as a parable. It may have happened. It probably did. Jesus began by saying, "There was a rich man" (Luke 16:19). He also introduced a poor, ill beggar. Inevitable death came for each of them. Now we learn more about each man than his state of economy and condition of health. Lazarus, the beggar, was a man of faith. The rich fellow is not pictured as a dishonest or immoral man. He probably was not. Still, he was not a man of faith. Apparently he was a this-world man who had no inclination or time for God. He had left God out, so now God was forced to leave him out.

The Bible describes the condition of both men immediately after death. Lazarus was carried to "Abraham's bosom" (Luke 16:22), a Jewish description of heaven. The other man was in hades, in torment crying, "I am in agony in this flame" (Luke 16:23-24).

This case history informs us of two addresses for the departed, each of which is determined by whether individuals place their faith in Jesus Christ. Knowing Christ makes all the difference in this world and the world to come. When pondering life after death, we always need to turn to God's Word. It shows us that those who have accepted His love and those who have ignored it have drastically different destinies.

Both destinies share some things in common. Each involves a period of time without a body. At death our bodies begin a process of returning to the earth. When Christ returns, our bodies will be resurrected and joined with our spirits. In 2 Corinthians 5, Paul spoke of life on earth as dwelling in a tent or tabernacle. After the resurrection we will not have temporary tents to live in but eternal buildings (bodies). Between death and the bodily resurrection is a time of being alive and conscious, yet without a body. It is a conscious, spiritual existence. Paul described this as an unfulfilled, incomplete experience; yet rewards or punishments already have begun.

After death, all are alive and conscious; and their eternal condition already is irrevocably determined.

At death, destiny for both the saved and the lost is set and fixed. Opportunity to decide already has passed. The man in hades was told his condition was fixed and could not be changed. After death, all are alive and conscious; and their eternal condition already is irrevocably determined.

We can note also some vast differences. When Lazarus, the man of faith, died, he immediately found himself in Abraham's bosom. The dying thief on the cross was assured that on the day of his death he would be with Christ in "Paradise" (Luke 23:43). Wherever Jesus went at the moment of His death, the thief joined Him. In Revelation 2:7, heaven is described as the "Paradise of God."

When Christians die, they go immediately to be with God. In 1 Thessalonians 4:14 we are told that at the Lord's return God will bring with Him those who have "fallen asleep" (a euphemism for death). In Philippians 1:23, Paul spoke of departing to be with Christ. His missionary life was one of great hardship, but he was bolstered by the knowledge that to leave this life was to go immediately into Christ's presence. Paul closed the great eighth chapter of Romans confidently declaring his assurance that death could not separate him from the Lord.

A terrible experience awaits those who die without Jesus Christ. They go immediately to a place called "Hades"—a place of punishment. The man said, "I am in agony in this flame" (16:24). The Bible declares that the Lord knows how "to keep the unrighteous under punishment for the day of judgment" (2 Pet. 2:9).

These are hard things for me to say; yet they must be said. It is hard for a doctor to tell a patient he or she has a cancerous tumor; yet it must be said so something can be done. The Great Physician lovingly diagnosed our case, discovered the malignancy of sin, and did what no earthly physician can do. He underwent the surgery for us. In fact, He died for you and me. His Word assures us of total forgiveness if only we will repent and turn to Him in faith.

Some people say, "Preacher, do not preach hell to us. A loving God would not send anyone to a place like that." God has done everything possible to keep peo-

ple out of hell. He sent His only Son to die for us. He pleads with us not to reject Christ. He consistently shows He loves us. He does not send anyone to hell. People do it themselves by saying no to Him. People send themselves by continuing in sin.

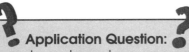

Application Question:
How do unsaved people you know respond to the concept of sin?
How has the community's view of sin changed over your lifetime?

Suppose a family living next door to you was starving to death—two little emaciated children, the mother, and the father all dying of malnutrition. You go to their house three times a day. You leave food and clothing for them. You bring a doctor to offer them medical help. You offer to pay all medical and hospital bills to help them back to health. They turn it all down. Finally they die. Someone comes and says to you, "How could you let those people die? You are a heartless neighbor!"

"But I did everything I could," you protest. "They would not let me help them."

Our Lord has knocked time and again at your heart's door. "I love you," He says. "I died for you. Please let me save you. *Please* let me save you. See these scars; they are for you." Oh, dear friend, understand the urgency. Do not go another minute without Christ. He did not come to send you to hell. He came so you would not have to go there.

Application Question:
Have you lately thanked God for His sacrifice of Christ on your behalf? Write out a brief prayer of thanksgiving:

Learning Activity 2

YOUR STORY

Prepare to tell your story of being saved by answering the following questions:

1. What was your life like before you knew Jesus as Lord?

2. What circumstances brought you to realize your need for Jesus?

3. When, where, and how did you receive Jesus as Lord?

4. What practical difference does Jesus make in your life day by day?

---

[1]James Cox, *Best Sermons 1* (New York: Harper and Row Publishers, 1988), 217.

[2]Ibid.

[3] John Bartlett, *Familiar Quotations,* 15th Edition (Boston: Little, Brown and Company, 1980), 626.

[4]Although some believe Luke 16:19-31 contains a factual account rather than a parable, it is included in this study because of its important teachings concerning the urgency of salvation. Whether or not it is a parable, it still teaches the reality of heaven, hell, and eternal punishment and reward.

CHAPTER

3

WHAT DOES IT MEAN TO FOLLOW CHRIST TODAY?

SCRIPTURE
VERSES

- Luke 14:25-33

Often in the Gospels we read about crowds of people following Jesus. Some were committed to Him; many were curious about Him; others simply wanted to be where the action was. Jesus wanted people to understand what it truly meant to be His follower. We need to make sure we hear Him and understand what it means to be His follower today.

One day Jesus was on His way to Jerusalem. He was not alone. The apostles were there, of course, and "great multitudes were going along with Him" (Luke 14:25). People love a crowd. Have you noticed? If you have a big crowd, more people will come. If you have a small crowd, few people are attracted. That is human nature.

Jesus loved the multitudes. He cried over Jerusalem's straying multitudes (Matt. 23:37). More than once He fed a multitude of people (Matt. 14:21; 15:29-39). Sometimes, however, Jesus gave the impression that He did not want large crowds following Him. Indeed, the larger the crowd, the more narrow His teachings. Jesus' teaching one day was so hard to accept that many of His disciples turned away. Jesus asked the twelve, "You do not want to go away also, do you?" (John 6:67).

On this day, to a big crowd of people Jesus spoke the words recorded in Luke 14:26-33. Take a moment to read this passage; then ask yourself, What is going on here? Other teachers would have spoken in broad generalities to the vast audience. Why did not Jesus make some nice comments designed to help the people feel better?

Making terminally ill people comfortable is the legitimate, primary function of a hospice. Helping ill people to regain health is the primary function of a hospital. Jesus' purpose was more that of the hospital than the hospice. He was not interested in entertaining or gaining a reputation as one who could draw huge crowds. He wanted to help people face reality about themselves and about sin and about God. To do that, He spoke truth. In Luke 14:26-33, He was speaking foundational truths.

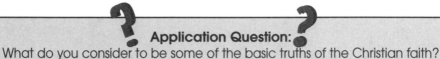

Application Question:
What do you consider to be some of the basic truths of the Christian faith?

Our Lord's words were demanding and concise because He was teaching the foundation facts of our faith. Any good builder will tell you the foundation must be solid. You cannot compromise the foundation.

On the campus of Ohio State University is the Wexner Art Center. The building has no pattern. Staircases go nowhere. Pillars support nothing. The building is described as being "designed in the postmodernist view of reality." The architect said he designed the building to reflect life. It goes nowhere and is mindless and senseless. The architect could plan and build "postmodern mindlessness" into the building itself, but he could not do that with the foundation. If he had designed the foundation as he did the rest of the structure, it all would have fallen down.

Jesus was dealing with the foundation. He had been teaching about the kingdom of God. Now our Lord Christ was answering some questions like: What do I do to be saved? What is salvation? What does it take to be a disciple of Christ? How do I enter God's kingdom? How do I have eternal life?

Foundation of Grace and Faith

Although the words *grace* and *faith* are not used in Luke 14:25-27, Jesus was telling about the necessary ingredients to enter the kingdom of God. "For by grace you have been saved through faith" (Eph. 2:8).

In grace God is acting. Our response to His grace is our faith.

We are saved by grace. In the parable of the great supper (14:15-24), grace is the central teaching. The invitation was extended, "Come; for everything is ready now" (Luke 14:17). The people who eventually came to the party were not the people you would expect to be there. They had done nothing to earn or deserve the invitation. They were there by the grace of the one giving the banquet. The lesson is that we are saved by grace alone. In grace God is acting. Our response to His grace is faith. We are saved by faith alone. Faith is our reaction to God's action of grace.

To follow Christ today means to place our faith in Him. Let's explore further what placing faith in Jesus means.

How do we do faith? What is faith? How does it work? These are the questions Jesus answered in our text. Faith is loving Him more than any other person. Faith is following Him instead of taking any other way. Faith is wanting Him more than any other thing.

Faith Is Loving Christ More Than Any Other Person

"If anyone comes to Me, and does not hate his own father and mother and wife and children and brothers and sisters, yes, and even his own life, he cannot be My disciple"(Luke 14:26).

> **Application Questions:**
> Imagine you are witnessing to a person who is enthusiastically investigating faith in Jesus. Would you quote Luke 14:26 to them? Why?

These difficult words do not sound like Jesus, do they? They do not even sound like the Bible. Sacred things are taught using family terms. God is our loving Father. We are

His children. Jesus is our joint heir, our brother. Husbands are told to love their wives as much as Christ loved the church (Eph. 5:25). Husbands are to "love their own wives as their own bodies" (Eph. 5:28). Wives are told to respect, to hold in high esteem, their husbands (Eph. 5:33). "Children, obey your parents in the Lord, for this is right. Honor your father and mother" (Eph. 6:1-2).

What do these words about hating one's family mean? The harsh conditions named here have caused much despair and confusion. Jesus was not contradicting the rest of God's Word about family love and respect. He was employing a dramatic means of teaching commonly used in His day. An emphatic way of saying someone loved one person more than another was to say that the person loved one and hated the other.

Application Question:
On the basis of your daily behavior, would others determine one of your relationships is more important to you than your relationship to Jesus Christ? If so, which one?

The parallel passage in Matthew reads, "He who loves father or mother more than Me is not worthy of Me; and he who loves son or daughter more than Me is not worthy of Me" (Matt. 10:37). The command is simply to put all other relationships on the altar of commitment to Christ. When we love Him in that way, a wondrous thing happens. We discover with Paul that being a bond-servant (slave) of Jesus Christ makes us free (Rom. 1:1). In like manner, when we love Christ more than husband, wife, father, mother, and brother or sister, we discover a greater ability to love these family members than ever before.

I know the gospel I preach changes people because I saw it change my father. He was 64 at the time of his decision to receive Christ. One of the major indications of his new life in Christ was his renewed love for my mother. A big part of faith in Christ is loving Him more than any other person.

Faith Is Following Him Instead of Any Other Way

"Whoever does not carry his own cross and come after Me cannot be My disciple" (Luke 14:27). What does it mean for one to carry his or her own cross? What does it mean to come after Jesus? We can only offer suggestions. These statements are as deep as the love of God.

Carrying Our Cross

The cross of Christ was the greatest revelation of God's love. "For God so loved the world, that He gave His only begotten Son" (John 3:16). "God demonstrates His own love toward us, in that while we were yet sinners, Christ died for us" (Rom. 5:8). Carrying the cross daily must mean that we carry with us the knowledge of God's great love for us.

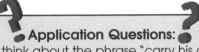

Application Questions:
When you think about the phrase "carry his own cross" (Luke 14:27), what images come to your mind?

The cross was also the most convincing condemnation of sin. When we look at the cross, we see sin revealed in all its ugliness. Sin is so cruel that it killed the Son of God. Our sin is so terrible that only His death could atone for it.

When we carry the cross, we carry to our world both the love of God and the condemnation of sin. The cross we carry inspires us to love people who do not want to be loved. The cross causes us to suffer because of the sins of the world. As soon as we make Christ our Savior, we begin to see our sin as He sees it. We become aware of what sin is doing to our world. The cross is doing something about sin.

To carry the cross is to carry the gift of salvation. We deliver to our world the love of God when we carry the cross. We take also the fact of sin's serious significance. These two truths meet and offer the gift of God's great salvation. Surely part of what is meant to carry the cross is to take God's offer of salvation to the world.

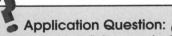

Application Question:
What are some people, policies, or principles you follow on a daily basis?

Following Jesus

To believe in Christ is to follow or obey Him. A major part of faith is following Him. "My sheep hear My voice, and I know them, and they follow Me" (John 10:27). The way of our Lord is always good. Our Christ gives His best to those who leave the choices with Him.

Knowing the will of God is difficult for some. Our responsibility as Christians is to seek and surrender to the will of God. This search is individual and private. God calls us to commitment and service in personal and unique ways.

F. B. Meyer described his call and surrender to "come after" our Lord. He sat dejectedly in his study. He said to himself, "My ministry is unfruitful, and I lack spiritual power."

> Christ said, "If you cannot trust me in all rooms of your life, I cannot accept any of the keys."

"Suddenly Christ seemed to stand beside him. 'Let me have the keys to your life,' Christ said. The experience was so real that he reached into his pockets and took out a bunch of keys! 'Are all the keys here?' 'Yes, Lord. All except the key to one small room in my life.' Christ said, 'If you cannot trust me in all rooms of your life, I cannot accept any of the keys.'

"Dr. Meyer was so overwhelmed with the feeling that Christ was moving out of his life because he was excluding Him from one interest in his life that he cried out, 'Come back, Lord, and take the keys to all the rooms of my life!'"[1]

Faith is following Him instead of any other way.

Application Question:
Is there a small room in your life, the keys to which you have not yet surrendered to Jesus? If so, what would happen if you gave Jesus that key too?

Faith Is Wanting Him More Than Any Other Thing

"So therefore, no one of you can be My disciple who does not give up all his own possessions" (Luke 14:33). This spirit of self-sacrifice asks, Are you willing to recognize that what you own is not yours? Do you see that nothing that can be lost is really owned? No one is wealthy to whom the grave brings bankruptcy.

This third condition for following Christ as His disciple causes us to be willing to say good-bye to things to which we will say good-bye anyway. You have never seen a funeral procession in which the hearse was pulling a trailer piled high with the deceased person's belongings. You, too, will say good-bye to the stuff one day.

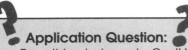

Application Question:
My head says, Everything belongs to God! What do my words and actions say?

Life's highest wisdom is not to attach our priorities to what we cannot keep but rather to give our devotion to Him whom we cannot lose. Ironically, the stuff of life is enjoyed most by those who know they are simply managing God's property for a while.

I have a friend who grew up on a Texas farm. He served in the infantry during World War II and faced combat in Europe. During that time of fighting, he had to spend long hours in a foxhole. He thought about his home and about farming. One dark night he pondered the fact that irrigation farming was coming and that meant there would be a need for specialized equipment and better seeds.

My friend came back from the war with a vision of a chain of farm and seed stores, but he had no money. For several years he coached and taught school and saved money. His wife also taught school. When they had saved $5,000, he and another man started a business that made them both millionaires. It stretched across the plains of Texas and even overseas. I would meet with this man and others about 6:00 a.m. at a little cafe. He was preoccupied, apparently unhappy and worried. The vastness of his business empire was a constant weight upon his shoulders.

Then suddenly he was a different man. He told us he had sold his business to a giant corporation, and they had hired him to stay in control. He still had the same job, managing the same business, sitting at the same desk, working with the same people. Knowing him, I'm sure he did not let up in dedication to that business one bit. He was a much happier man because he was a manager rather than an owner. Now he was watching over something backed by the brainpower and financial power of a giant corporation. It was no longer just his baby.

A lot of pressure is taken off us when we realize we are tending to God's things, not ours. With the resources of the Creator behind us, we cannot fail.

Summary

On the foundation of God's grace we build our discipleship. We are saved by grace. It all begins with the action of God. He offers us His free salvation. We are saved through faith. Faith is our part. It is our response to His act of grace. Faith means loving Him more than any other person. Faith means following Him instead of any other way. Faith means wanting Him more than any other thing. Simply put, you must be willing to take what is dearest to you—whether people, plans, or property—and kiss it good-bye. This is how you become a disciple of Jesus Christ. This is how you enter the kingdom of God. This is what it means to follow Jesus today.

Counting the Cost

Jesus told two parables to underline the cost of following Him. Many people hesitate to commit themselves fully to Christ in faith because they fear the cost of doing so.

Learning Activity 1
WHAT DOES IT MEAN TO FOLLOW JESUS BY FAITH?

1. _____ is loving Him more than any other person.

2. Faith is _____ Him instead of any other way.

3. Faith is wanting _____ more than any other _____.

The best thing on TV one night was a Billy Graham Crusade. That is true any night a Billy Graham Crusade is on television. In his sermon Dr. Graham told of visiting a leader of a large denomination. The leader said, "I do not really know that I am saved. Can you tell me how I can know I am right with God?" Billy Graham said when he left that man's office, the man was smiling through tears of joy because he knew he was saved.

"Pressure is taken off when we realize we are looking after God's things, not ours."

YOUR NOTES

(LUKE 14:25-33)

BSSB PHOTO

Then the great evangelist told how he was asked to visit Dwight D. Eisenhower in his hospital room in Washington. President Eisenhower was spending the last days of his life in that hospital room and he knew it. He said, "Billy, would you go over with me what I need to know to be sure I am saved." Dr. Graham said, "I will never forget leaving that room, looking back at Ike Eisenhower smiling that winning smile of his because he knew he was right with God."

As Billy Graham told these stories, I was moved. I remembered a similar experience with someone more important than a denominational leader or even a president. I will never forget the day my mother looked me in the eye and said, "Son, can you tell me how I can know that I am saved?" I opened the Word of God to her and the sweet Holy Spirit assured her of her salvation.

In this fourteenth chapter of Luke, Christ was teaching how we can be saved, that is, how we can enter the kingdom of God. He said the kingdom of God is like a banquet; and the invitation is extended "Come; for everything is ready now" (Luke 14:17). This picture of the kingdom of God as a banquet appears in the closing words of the Bible. John heard a voice say, "Write, 'Blessed are those who are invited to the marriage supper of the Lamb'" (Rev. 19:9).

❓ Application Questions: ❓

What is the biggest price you pay for following Jesus?

What would be the biggest price you would pay for not following Jesus?

All of us are invited. Our salvation is an act of God's grace. It is freely and totally given by a grace act of the loving God. Grace means unmerited favor. God offers you eternal life that can never be deserved or earned.

Learning Activity 2
FOLLOWING JESUS: MY COST
For each category write a brief sentence that describes your cost to follow Jesus.
Time:

Family:

Friends:

Finances:

Recreation:

Vocation:

God's Cost for Me to Follow Jesus: His Only Son

Our reaction to God's action of grace is faith. Faith is the way we receive His grace. "For by grace you have been saved through faith; . . . it is the gift of God" (Eph. 2:8). We have in Luke 14 a description of saving faith. Faith is loving Him more than any other person (Luke 14:26). Faith is following Him instead of any other way (14:27). Faith is loving Him more than any other thing (14:33).

The question is, Can you afford *not* to follow Him (Christ)?

You may say, "That is a big price." No, it is not. The price is not large when you compare it to what you pay if you do not come by faith to Christ. The question is *not,* Can you afford to follow Christ? The question is, Can you afford *not* to follow Him? That is the cost to count.

Building a Life (Luke 14:28-30)

The builder of a tower ponders, *Do I have the resources and materials to build the building I want?* The builder of a life wonders, *Do I have the resources and materials to build the life I really want?* Do you? What kind of life do you want? How long do you want it to last? What goals do you want to accomplish? How will you handle guilt? How will you handle life's inevitable failures? Where will you find inner strength to face the jolts of life? Do you have the moral fiber to avoid the pitfalls that can make life ineffective?

> The fact is, none of us has the materials and resources in ourselves to live well in this world.

Many marriages have failed because of the absence of moral fiber. This is not a judgment of any individual situation. This is a general statement but it is true. The same is true of employment terminations. Now there are numerous economic factors out of anyone's control that cause job termination. Yet an amazing number of jobs and businesses are lost, not because the employees or the employers did not do the job well, but because they could not live well. The fact is, none of us has the materials and resources in ourselves to live well in this world. "For all have sinned"—missed the mark and fallen short (Rom. 3:23).

Another question to you, life builder, How do you handle the fact that each day you are moving closer to your eternal destiny? "It is appointed for men to die once, and after this comes judgment" (Heb. 9:27). Are you ready for that? Count the cost.

Jesus gives us truth on which we can build a life.

Our Lord's Sermon on the Mount (Matt. 5—7) is about happy, joyous, effective living. Jesus closed that message with a warning. If we do not hear what He tells us and do it, we are like a foolish carpenter who built his house on a foundation of sand. When life's storms roll in and the wind blows, it collapses like a house of cards. If we hear and heed His words, we find they are foundational

"First sit down and calculate the cost" (Luke 14:28).

words. Jesus gives us truth on which we can build a life. When we have come to Him by faith, none of life's winds or waves or tornadoes can move us. We are built upon the rock. We are anchored, fixed to that rock.

The question is *not* Can I afford to turn by faith to Christ? The question is Can I afford not to? Only He has the resources we need to live.

Winning Life's War (14:31-33)

Another question is, Do you and I have the strength and power to win life's war? In my 60-plus years of living, one thing has been a constant. All my life a war has been going on somewhere. I do not believe a day has passed that soldiers were not fighting and killing one another somewhere. The Bible says, "You will be hearing of wars and rumors of wars" (Matt. 24:6). That has been true, I know, for the past 60 years.

> The Bible declares spiritual forces are trying to destroy us.

Ask any teenage student about terror and war. In school they have learned about the ominous power of a split atom. On television they have been confronted with raging masses in rebellion. Live pictures of war are shown in color, demonstrating the hatred of people determined to exterminate one another.

The same teenager, like any of us, also recognizes there is war within us. Evil lurks in the hearts of human beings—there is no doubt. Opposing powers pull us in opposite directions. The Bible declares spiritual forces are trying to destroy us. "For our struggle is not against flesh and blood, but against the rulers, against the powers, against the world forces of this darkness, against the spiritual forces of wickedness in the heavenly places" (Eph. 6:12).

Our enemy is named and identified, "Your adversary, the devil, prowls about like a roaring lion, seeking someone to devour" (1 Pet. 5:8). The consistent message of the Bible is that we do not in and of ourselves have the power to win against such an enemy.

> We must not underestimate our adversary.

A president many years ago had a dog that constantly picked fights with other dogs, and he was always beaten. One day a friend of the president said, "Your dog is not much of a fighter, is he?" "On the contrary," said the president. "He is a great fighter, but he always underestimates his adversary." We must not underestimate our adversary.

 Application Question:
In what circumstance have you recently underestimated your spiritual adversary? Describe what happened and your related feelings.

When we come by faith to Jesus Christ, we have in Him the resources to fight our dreaded enemy. We are issued the full armor so we can stand against the schemes of the devil (Eph. 6:11-18). Jesus demonstrated His power in His earthly ministry. Mary Magdalene was possessed by demons and was delivered from the enemy by Jesus Christ. A man literally living in tombs was released from demonic powers by Jesus Christ. Lazarus was called back even from death's clutches by the Lord Christ.

Jesus is still delivering people from the enemy. A pastor friend told of a new convert who came to his office. The man said, "You have not said anything about money. How much should I give to the church?" The pastor told him about the tithe. "What a great deal," the new convert said. "My whiskey and gambling used to cost more than that."

When Jesus is our Savior, the ultimate victory is ours. When the climactic battle of history is fought between Jesus Christ and Satan, it will not be a drawn-out battle with many casualties on each side. Our Lord Christ simply will speak the word, and Satan and his armies will be defeated (Rev. 19:19-21).

We will win the spiritual war and find lasting peace when we come by faith to Jesus Christ. My friend, count the cost. You cannot afford to face the forces of evil without Jesus Christ.

The act of faith is often described as "taking the plunge." Can you picture this? You are on a ledge standing on the edge of decision. Before you is the deep, clean water of eternal life. Behind and around you are the things, thoughts, and people—the influences—that have guided your life.

You look at yourself and see what you have suppressed or failed to see before. You see the grime and filth you have collected from the foul and polluted places you have been. There are even cakes of dried blood, the consequences of wrong decisions, you cannot wash off.

Jesus Christ is standing beside you. "What do I do?" you ask Him. "Dive, let yourself go." "I would rather jump." "No, you must dive. If you jump trying to protect yourself, you will fail to go deep enough. If you try to save your own life, you will lose it. Trust me. Dive."

> The act of faith is often referred to as "taking the plunge."

You say, "It looks like a long way down to the water. I may die. Lord, have you brought me to this place to die?" "Trust me," He says. "Take the plunge. You will die if you do not. Take the plunge."

An appealing, cultured voice from the shadows rings out. "Nonsense. You will not die if you refuse to take the plunge." You turn to see this enormously impressive person. He is everything the world tells us we should be. This person has the beauty of movie actress or the ability of a professional athlete, the business bearing of the president of a Fortune-500 company, and the sensual power of a popular singer. He is a conglomerate of the best of this fallen world. He is the devil.

"Think," says the devil. "Think of all the good times you have had. Are you going to leave those behind? What will your family think? What will your friends say? Do you know what lies ahead if you follow Jesus? Think of the money you can make, the things you can own. Will you give all that up for something you are not sure of?"

You have heard that pitch many times before. In fact, all your life you have followed "Old Red Legs" who let you think you were in charge (Eph. 2:1-3). You look again at the resulting grime and filth and blood. You look hard at the stains and pains of the self-centered life.

You turn to Jesus and say to Him, "I give myself to love You most so I can love others more—indeed, so I can love myself more. I yield myself to follow You because Your way is what I would want if I knew as much as You. I declare my relationship with You to be my most precious possession. I trust You to give me everything I need." And you plunge into life—headfirst and heart-first, forever.

The way of our Lord is always good. Our Christ gives His best to those who leave the choices with Him, to those who follow Him in truth.

---

[1]Paul Lee Tan, *Encyclopedia of 7,700 Illustrations: Signs of the Times* (Rockville, Maryland: Assurance Publishers, 1985), 7. Used by permission.

WHAT DOES GOD EXPECT OF US?

SCRIPTURE VERSES

∎**Luke 16:1-13; 19:11-27**

I had traveled all the way to New York City to talk to him about preaching. Sitting in his living room, I was thrilled to be visiting with one of the most effective media ministers of all time. When television was young, he appeared on prime time Sunday evenings teaching the Bible. He was fully sponsored by Admiral Corporation. His broadcasts appeared opposite Frank Sinatra and Milton Berle, the biggest stars of his day. His audience was 15-20 million viewers. In 1952 the Academy of Television Arts and Sciences named Fulton Sheen the most outstanding personality on television.

Fulton Sheen looked at me with those famous penetrating eyes and said, "You have come to New York City to talk to me about preaching? I cannot talk to you about preaching. I do not know what to say. Preaching is a gift. It is like being a beautiful woman. She is not responsible for having her beauty, but she is very responsible for what she does with it."

All we have are gifts from God. Our time, our talents, our resources all are gifts. Like beauty and brilliance, we are not responsible for having them; but we are responsible for what we do with them. Our salvation, our lives are gifts of God's grace. The Bible teaches that God expects Christians to manage these gifts in ways that will gain for us unlimited, unfading, guaranteed riches.

Bad Man, Good Example (Luke 16:1-13)

This title is the theme of one of Jesus' more puzzling parables. Our Lord told His disciples (this parable is not for people who are not Christians) about a rich man who had a slave. The slave acted as the rich man's steward, a role like Joseph's in Potiphar's household (Gen. 39:1-6). The steward was responsible for managing his master's vast holdings. Someone suggested to the rich man that his steward was mishandling the money, squandering it, spending the money indiscriminately. The steward was called on the carpet and told to settle his affairs, get the books in order, and get out.

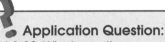

Application Question:
Read Luke 16:1-13. What questions come to your mind as you seek to understand the message Jesus was communicating in this parable? Write them here:

In wide-eyed panic, this dishonest manager began to ponder his future. *What in the world will I do? I am too lazy to work. I am too proud to beg. What will I do?* The wheels in his brain began to turn counterclockwise. His brain's wheels were conditioned to turn in the wrong direction. His mind, greased by greed and expediency, worked rapidly. He thought

How much do you owe?

SARAH FOSTER

to himself, *I have it! I will call in my master's debtors and reduce their debts, falsi-fying their accounts. Then because I have helped them, they will be obligated to help me. If they do not feel obligated enough, I will have material for blackmail because they will have a part in the crime.*

He called the debtors in one by one. *How much do you owe?*

One hundred measures of oil.

Then change it to fifty, said the steward. Another debtor came to his desk, *What is your debt?*

One hundred measures of wheat, he answered.

Then take the pen and write down eighty. And so it went.

Application Question:
When someone you know gets affirmed by a superior for doing something unethical, how do you respond?

When the master discovered this trickery, he was . . . well, he was impressed. Surely he was disturbed, certainly he was angry, and the steward did lose his job. Still, the master also was impressed. Jesus, the author of this story, said there is something in the bad man's action that is a good example. He said in effect, *This fellow is a shrewd dude. He is a crook, but he is clever in a way you need to emulate.*

Learning Activity 1
THE PARABLE OF THE DISHONEST STEWARD

(1) List the possible truths from this parable.

(2) Write one sentence describing the main point of this parable.

What is the lesson of this puzzling parable? It is this: Life as the steward had experienced it would soon be over. His days as a free-wheeling spender of another man's wealth were ending. So, he took steps to prepare for living beyond that abrupt ending.

> No matter how much or how little you may have in ability, opportunity, or wealth, you can manage your life so as to be really rich.

Lessons in Life Management

In this setting our Lord taught us lessons in life management. Here is His emphasis: No matter how much or how little you may have in ability, opportunity, or wealth, you can manage your life so as to be really rich.

Application Question:
Read Ephesians 1:3-14. What one-sentence prayer comes to mind in light of those verses? Write it here:

If you would be truly successful, you must know that all you have, you have by the grace of God. God expects you to learn and live by the laws of life management; then you will reap the rewards of life management.

> Life management is not about getting in heaven.... Life management is about usefulness on earth and rewards in heaven.

Foundation of God's Grace

The principles of life management are built on the solid foundation of the grace of Almighty God. In Ephesians 1:3-14 this foundation is spelled out in remarkable clarity. The Word declares we have been selected by the Father because He loves us. We have been saved by the Son, the Lord Jesus

Christ, who died on the cross because of that love. We have been sealed by the Holy Spirit, assured of our salvation forever because of the love and grace of our wonderful God. We can do nothing to save our souls except turn to God in repentance and faith in Jesus Christ. So, life management is not about getting into heaven. All who come to Christ will be in heaven. Life management is about usefulness on earth and rewards in heaven.

These life management principles or laws are only for Christians. They have to do with living life in such a way as to one day hear God say, *Well done, good and faithful servant. Because you have been faithful in a very little thing, you will be in authority over very much* (see Matt. 25:23). Successful living then demands that you know and keep the laws of life management.

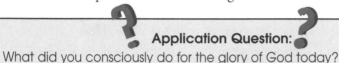

Application Question:
What did you consciously do for the glory of God today?

Laws of Life Management

Law No. 1: Do your best with what you have. It does not matter in God's eyes how much you have but how well you handle it. Barnabas's large gift of land to the early church was deemed significant enough to be recorded in Scripture (Acts 4:36-37). A widow was lauded by our Lord for her gift of less than a penny (Luke 21:3). Someone said, "I am but one, but I am one. I cannot do much, but I can do something. What I can do, I ought to do. What I ought to do, by the grace of God, I will do."

The Bible commands, "Whatever you do, do all to the glory of God" (1 Cor.10:31). I heard about a tombstone on a shoe cobbler's grave in a Scottish cemetery. It declares that for 50 years he had cobbled shoes to the glory of God.

Rest in Peace

For fifty years he cobbled shoes to the glory of God.

ILLUSTRATION BY RICK BURTON

Luke 16:10 says, "He who is faithful in a very little thing is faithful also in much." If you are honest in the little things, you will be honest in the big things. If you are not honest in little jobs, you will never be put in charge of the store. The first law of life management: Do your best with what you have.

Law No. 2: What we manage is not ours. A while back I read of a strange thief. There was not a single brick, tile, screw, or nail in his neat little house that had not been stolen. Over a period of a couple of years and by way of many different thefts, he acquired every square inch of his house at someone else's expense. He even admitted he had stolen the flowers blooming in his front yard. Day by day, bit by bit, he accomplished his theft.

That thief's actions parallel the spiritually crippled behavior of many people. Day by day they appropriate the things of God—His air, His sunshine, His food. They take everything He gives and use all for selfish purposes. Actually they embezzle life because they give nothing in return. In building their lives, every single brick, tile, screw, and nail is stolen.

> Because that which can be lost is not really owned, then not even our lives belong to us.

All of us arc like the steward, temporarily handling the property of another. "The earth is the Lord's," declares the Bible, "and all it contains" (Ps. 24:1). Because that which can be lost is not really owned, then not even our lives belong to us. The steward was a slave. He belonged to His master. Likewise, "In Him we live and move and exist" (Acts 17:28). Life, breath, and all things come from Him.

Application Question:
What does it mean to use things for a selfish purpose? Give an example.

Our time, our talents, our resources are all God's, given by His grace, controlled by His providence. If we are Christians,

we have accepted that He is our loving Master and that we will give an accounting to Him.

> How sad to see people steal a life from the Master and then realize they are stuck with what they stole.

How sad to see people steal a life from the Master and then realize they are stuck with what they stole. I remember reading about people who have stolen from others, seemingly succeeded in getting away with their dishonesty, but then suffered—some greatly—as a result of their misdeeds. These people also have been stuck with what they stole. Others steal from their employers, often something minor or inexpensive, but get caught and lose their jobs. They too are stuck with what they stole. Have you ever read about or known people who have experienced this in their lives? Have you ever experienced yourself? A constant warning from God's Word is this: People who embezzle their lives from God are stuck with what they stole.

Life management is to do our best with what we have. It is to know that what we manage is not ours.

Law No. 3: The things we manage are not real. In verse 11 is a heavy question, *If you have not been trustworthy in handling worldly wealth, who will trust you with true riches?* "True" means authentic, genuine, permanent. The wealth of this world is not real because it does not last.

Application Questions:

Do you treat some temporary things in your life as though they are permanent? If so, describe one:

What change in attitude or approach should you make in this area of life management?

The goods we now manage are temporary. Life's largest blunder is to act as though this were not so. "Their inner thought is," said the psalmist, "that their houses are forever, and their dwelling places to all generations. They have called their lands after their own names" (Ps. 49:11). This is sheer mockery. "For," as the Bible says of one who lusts after the treasures of earth, "when he dies he will carry nothing away" (Ps. 49:17).

Alexander the Great was born to one empire and con-quered another. He possessed the wealth of both the East and the West. Yet he commanded that when carried to his grave, his hands should be left unwrapped and outside the funeral bier so that all might see them empty.

The great Charlemagne, at his request, was buried sitting on his throne, wearing his crown, robe, and jewels. In his lap was an open Bible with one finger resting on Mark 8:36, "What does it profit a man to gain the whole world, and for-feit his soul." Successful life management is a matter of exchanging a life you cannot keep for a life you cannot lose. It is trading the temporary goods of this world for unending, secure treasure. No matter how much or how little you may have in ability, opportunity, or wealth, you can manage your life in such a way as to be really rich.

> Successful life management is a matter of exchanging a life you cannot keep for a life your cannot lose.

Taking Care of Business (Luke 19:11-27)
Since Luke 9:51, our Lord had been on His way to Jerusalem. It was a path to injustice, painful beating, soul agony, death, resurrection, and heaven. The truth for all of us is that heaven is on the other side of the cross.

> *Now hear this. This is why I came to earth. I came to seek and to save the lost.*

The crowd following Him had just witnessed an amazing thing (19:1-10). Jesus had seen Zaccheus up in a tree. He called him by name and went home with him. Those who did not know soon learned that Zaccheus was quite rich and bit-terly hated because he collected taxes for the Roman govern-ment. After a time with Jesus, Zaccheus made a public procla-mation. He announced he was giving away half his wealth and making four-fold restitution to anyone he had cheated. Jesus said of him, *He is acting like this because he has been saved. He has learned who he is. Now hear this. This is why I came to earth. I came to seek and to save the lost* (see 16:9-10).

The crowd did not think that was why Jesus had come. They had to be corrected because they were on a collision course with deep disappointment. Ever since they had learned Jesus was on His way to Jerusalem, the crowd had become more and more excited. Now Jerusalem was just a few miles away. Jerusalem was what they had been waiting for.

His disciples were saying to themselves, *The time has come. We have followed Him all these months. We have heard teaching that could come only from the heart of God. He has healed the incurable. He has cast out demons. We have seen the spell of sin broken. We have seen the look in the grateful eyes of those to whom He has given new life. He has even gone into the realm of death to bring people back. Now things are coming to a head. For these past few weeks He has made clear His determined goal of going to Jerusalem. Surely He will claim the throne of David. We will be free again. We will no longer be oppressed by the great Roman beast.*

Jesus knew His disciples and many other people were thinking these things, and He knew what actually would take place in Jerusalem. Instead of a political takeover, there would be an execution. They would not experience the light of giddy freedom and victory, but the dark of Calvary's apparent defeat. They would be crushed. Many of them would lose faith. The same excited and adoring crowds that would welcome Him into Jerusalem would demand His death.

> The ultimate realization of the kingdom was far in the future. In the meanwhile, there was work for the citizens of the kingdom.

"And while they were listening to these things, He went on to tell a parable, because He was near Jerusalem, and they supposed that the kingdom of God was going to appear immediately" (19:11). They needed to know that the kingdom in all its fullness and glory was not going to appear in just a few days. In fact, the ultimate realization of the kingdom was far in the future. In the meanwhile, there was work for the citizens of the kingdom. There is a task God expects His people to be doing until the King comes again in victory.

What Happened?

With all this in mind, Jesus told a parable about a nobleman who went away to receive His kingdom. Before leaving on his journey, the nobleman called 10 servants to him and gave to each one of them a "mina." A mina was worth about three months wages for labor in the field or in the marketplace. It was not a fortune, but it was no small amount either. The nobleman instructed his servants, "Do business with this until I come back" (Luke 19:13).

Many citizens in the land hated the nobleman. They did not want him to be their king, so they sent a delegation to try to prevent his coronation. The servants in Jesus' parable would find doing business for the master difficult because he had so many enemies.

Jesus' listeners likely knew some of their kings had gone to Rome to receive the authority to rule. For example, not long after Jesus' birth, Archelaus had gone to Rome to secure part of Herod (his father) the Great's kingdom to rule. A delegation from the area had gathered in Rome to protest Archelaus's becoming their king.

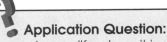

Application Question:
What is one area in your life where it is difficult to be about Jesus' business because of those who are enemies of His kingdom? Describe it here:

One of the slaves worked so hard and so faithfully he multiplied by 10 the master's mina. Another earned 5 more minas. Probably other slaves took advantage of the master's absence to use the mina to do business, not for him, but for themselves. One slave did nothing. He just wrapped the money in his handkerchief, put it in a safe place, and did his own thing.

One day the report began to circulate, The master is coming. He is just outside the gates. Those who did not love him were frightened and ran away. Those who loved him were thrilled and ran to see him. There he was, now a king. Probably he had with him an army of the most impressive and powerful-appearing soldiers imaginable.

That night the slaves were called in for an accounting. When the faithful, loyal slave showed his master, now the king, his ten minas, the king beamed with love and pride in his eyes. He said, "Well done, good slave, because you have been faithful in a very little thing, be in authority over ten cities" (19:17).

The slave whose business for the king had produced five minas was made ruler over five cities. One by one the servants came to report. The third slave we are told about had taken the master's mina and wrapped it in a handkerchief and hid it. He made his dismal report.

Application Questions:

What are some gifts of God you have invested and seen multiplied?

What are some gifts of God you have not yet used?

Some good can be found in the third slave's actions. At least he recognized that the mina was not his. It belonged to the master. He did not take what the master had given him and act as though it were his own. Apparently, though, he did not want to work on something that would not benefit himself. Whatever he made with the mina would belong to the master. He guarded the master's wealth, being careful not to lose it. His business activity was not the master's business, but his own.

That slave stood before the king and had either the courage or the stupidity to say, "Master, behold your mina, which I kept put away in a handkerchief; for I was afraid of you, because you are an exacting man; you take up what you did not lay down, and reap what you did not sow" (19:20-21).

The king replied in essence, *If that is how you think I am, then that is how I will treat you.* He ordered that the mina be taken away from the unproductive slave and given to the slave who had 10 minas.

Whether the next statement is in the parable or is a reaction to the people hearing Jesus tell the parable is not clear. "And they said to him, 'Master, he has ten minas already'" (19:25). They were told that is the way things are in the kingdom. Those who do good business get more, and those who do no business lose what they have.

The parable continues. The master's face suddenly took on a hard look. He was not dealing now with his slaves. He was dealing with those who refused His right to be king. "But these enemies of mine, who did not want me to reign over them, bring them here, and slay them in my presence" (19:27).

It is quite a story, is it not? No sweet little religious anecdote is this. Its setting, its content, and its implications are jolting, especially when we understand that the real King, who is one day coming again, is the Author.

Questions hammer at our heads for an answer: What is this business of the King? What are the minas, that with which we do business? In which of these groups will I find myself when the day of accounting comes? What does God expect of me?

What Is This Business of the King?

"Do business with this until I come back" (Luke 19:13). What is this business of the King? Do you want a good clue? Look at 19:10, "For the Son of Man has come to seek and to save that which was lost."

The organization that made the largest impact on my boyhood is Royal Ambassadors. We have a chapter of Royal Ambassadors in our church. The first stanza of the Royal Ambassadors' song ends with this line, "I'm here on business for my King." What is that business?

As the Father has sent Me, I also send you.

Hear these statements of our Lord: "I came that they might have life, and might have it abundantly" (John 10:10). "The Son of Man has come to seek and to save that which was lost" (Luke 19:10). The resurrected Christ appeared to His disciples and said, "As the Father has sent Me, I also send you" (John 20:21). He gave the Holy Spirit to them to empower them in that purpose. The last lines of Matthew's account of our Lord's life and teachings present the living, resurrected Lord saying to His disciples, "All authority has been given to Me in heaven and on earth. Go therefore and make disciples of all the nations, baptizing them in the name of the Father and the Son and the Holy Spirit, teaching them to observe all that I have commanded you; and lo, I am with you always, even to the end of the age" (Matt. 28:18-20).

Before His bodily return to heaven, Jesus called His followers together and told them "to wait for what the Father had promised, . . . the Holy Spirit" (Acts 1:4-5). They were still occupied with the kingdom idea. Their minds were not filled with thoughts of kingdom work but with wonder and dreams of majesty. So they asked, *Is this it, Lord? Are you restoring the kingdom to Israel?* (Acts 1:6). Jesus responded, *You do not need to know those things, but you do need to hear this: You will receive power when the Holy Spirit comes upon you and you will be My witnesses* (Acts 1:7-8). Then in the Book of Acts, the history of that beginning band of bold believers in Christ, we read that they did pray; they did receive the Holy Spirit; and they did witness.

What is this business of the King? It is to tell as many as we can about the love of God in Christ Jesus. God's people are not here to wring their hands and moan, "Look what the world is coming to." We are here joyfully to proclaim, "Look who has come to the world!"

> God's people are not here to wring their hands and moan, "Look what the world is coming to." We are here joyfully to proclaim, "Look who has come to the world!"

What Is Given Us with Which to Do Business?

The master gave each slave some working capital with which to do business. Each servant was given a mina. No one had more than any other. It was something that could be taken away. Losing it did not put the selfish servant in the same category as those who rejected the king's rule and reign. What does the mina mean in this story? What has been given to us with which to do our Lord's business?

The mina cannot stand for ability or talent. We do not all have the same amount of that. It certainly is not wealth or money. We are not on an even keel in the bank-account category. It is not charismatic personality. Some of us are bubbly and some of us are not. What is this equal gift we all have and with which we do His business? I think it is the gift of His salvation—the truth about Jesus Christ and the accompanying joy that comes from sharing it. The Book of Acts makes clear that if you make the first business of your life to honor Jesus Christ, you will have the fullness of the Spirit.

If you are observant, you readily will agree that serving the Lord brings rewards. Believers who serve only themselves quickly lose distinctive aspects of happiness, friendship, joy, peace, and quality of life. David recognized this relationship between joy and serving the Lord through witnessing. Remember how he prayed, "Restore to me the joy of Thy salvation. . . . Then I will I teach transgressors Thy ways" (Ps. 51:12-13).

When the King comes, all will be called to give an account to Him. For some, it will be a day of great joy, a gigantic reward. *Well done, good slave. You have been faithful over little things. Let me show you how rich you really are!* Sadly, the vast majority of people will be those who have refused to acknowledge Jesus as King. Their fate will be tragic and final.

All too many of us, I fear, are like that man who hid his mina. What are we to say about Christians who know salvation is important but never share it. They are doing their own business, not God's. They guard their salvation. They keep it tucked away in a secure place.

How many of us are like that? When the Master comes, we plan to get out His gift, unwrap it, and say, "Here it is, Lord. I got this from you and now I am cashing it in." Then we will realize what we have already lost. We will have lost the joy of serving God and the great rewards that could have been ours.

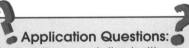

Application Questions:

When was the last time you talked with someone about the gift of God's salvation?

Regardless of the person's response, how did you feel?

These Christians are described in 1 Corinthians 3:11-15. They are believers. Jesus Christ is their Lord. That is the foundation for us all—our faith in Jesus Christ—but in selfish, careless living, they have built nothing spiritual or lasting upon that foundation. The fire of judgment will burn up every work, and yet the foundation will still be there. They will be saved by the skin of their teeth, but the potential of great reward will be gone forever.

YOUR NOTES

(LUKE 19:11-27)

Learning Activity 2
DEED

I, _____, do hereby deed
the sole possession of my estate to the control of Jesus of
Nazareth, understanding that He expects this of me. This estate
includes but is not limited to:

My favorite person

My favorite pastime

My favorite toy

My favorite dream

My bank account(s) with

My job at

I accept my new role as steward (manager) of that previously
thought to be mine. I now place priority on the business of the
new owner (Jesus of Nazareth) in bringing people into His
kingdom.

_____   _____
(Signature)   (Date)

CHAPTER

WHY DO WE GIVE UP ON PRAYER?

▪Luke 18:1-8

Our Lord was a splendid storyteller. His stories that put the grand truths of God in simple, everyday settings and served them on paper plates. His stories always had a purpose. One day He told a particular story to His disciples, those who believed in Him and followed Him. It is a simple story, therefore a good one. It is not like a Ludlum or Grisham novel with a long list of characters to keep up with. It has but two characters, a widow and a judge. Note the purpose of that story, "He was telling them a parable to show that at all times they ought to pray and not to lose heart" (Luke 18:1).

Application Question:
What is an area in your life where you feel you have absolutely no protection or support apart from God's protection and support?

Let's be honest at this point. We may not have given up on prayer, but we have at least been tempted to give up. After all, most of us have prayed many prayers that were not answered, at least not answered in the way we asked. We all have had the feeling at times that our prayers never got past the ceiling. Also, life's disappointments can devastate us and cause us to wonder whether God is really there or whether He really cares. Maybe that is the basic issue—to what kind of God do we pray? In this marvelous story, Jesus addressed that issue and more.

Learning Activity 1
LUKE 18:2-5
Use this page to take notes as your group discusses Luke 18:2-5.

THE WIDOW   BELIEVERS

THE JUDGE   GOD

THE WIDOW'S ACTION

PRAYER

The Widow

Widows show up a lot in Jesus' teaching and preaching. His world was dominated by men. A woman without a man's protection and support was vulnerable; she had virtually no protection and support. Our Lord's hardest teachings were against the religious leaders who used their positions to take what the poor wid-

ows had. He said they "devour widows' houses" (Luke 20:47; Mark 12:40). Jesus thought a lot about the plight of widows. In His parable, the woman was being bullied either criminally or bureaucratically. No one was on her side; no one would help her. Her only hope was the legal system.

The Judge

The widow went to see the judge. Now the plot thickens. The judge was as mean and heartless as she was weak and helpless. In two statements our Lord described him. He "did not fear God, and did not respect man" (Luke 18:2). He had neither reverence for God nor regard for people. Those two things go together, do they not? When asked about the greatest commandment, Jesus replied, " 'You shall love the Lord your God with all your heart, and with all your soul, and with all your mind.' This is the great and foremost commandment. And a second is like it, 'You shall love your neighbor as yourself' " (Matt. 22:37-39).

Loving God and loving our brothers and sisters is a package deal. You do not have one without the other.

Loving God and loving our brothers and sisters is a package deal. You do not have one without the other (1 John 3:14-17). This judge had love neither for God nor for others. He was as warm and loving as the inside of a refrigerator. He probably sent his mother a belated birthday card saying, "I didn't forget; I just didn't care." Tell him what the Bible says and he would reply, "So what?" Tell him what is right and wrong and he would laugh. Tell him he is accountable to God and he would scoff. In his mind and actions he did not serve the law; the law served him. Like Judge Roy Bean of Pecos, Texas, in frontier days, he *was* the law. To any plea for justice, he would respond, "Frankly, my dear, I just don't give a hoot."

Irony of ironies, the helpless widow's only hope for justice was this judge. She carefully rehearsed her appeal—rewriting and polishing it until she could state her problem with minimum words and maximum impact. When she stood before the judge the first time, he hardly acknowledged her presence. As she started her well-prepared appeal, he probably looked at his watch. When he realized she was asking for his help, he rolled his eyes and winked at a deputy. Before she had finished the first paragraph of her statement, he abruptly called to the bailiff, *Get her out of here!*

Application Questions:

Is a broken relationship with another believer currently hindering your prayer life? If so, with whom? _____ Read Matthew 5:23-24; 18:15; 1 Peter 3:7. What is one step you will take this week to correct the relationship?

As she was led away, she said, *But sir, you are my only hope!*

While his coworkers and cronies smiled at the idea of his being anyone's hope, the judge laughed. His laugh was the last thing she heard as the doors closed. She had thrown herself on the mercy of the court, but the court had no mercy.

The Strategy

No sense in dealing with that man any more, right? So it was over? Not quite. Now the plot clots. The widow was hurt, offended, rejected, desperate. What could she do? *That man is still my only hope,* she thought to herself. *I am going to force him to do something. He will either lock me up, put me away, or help me out.*

From that moment, she was on him like mustard on a hot dog. She was a constant whisper in his ear. She became as annoying as an itch you can't scratch and as disturbing as ink splattered on a new silk suit. Every time he turned around, he saw that widow. When the judge backed his Cadillac out of his driveway in the morning, there she was, waiting in her 12-year-old Chevy Nova. She chugged along behind him as he went to work. Anytime he was presiding in the courtroom, she was sitting on the back row. She matched his every step in the hall, talking to him about her case. When he came out of his office, she was standing there, talking about her case. When he went to lunch, she followed. She absolutely refused to give up.

It worked! One day the judge came out of his office and found himself looking at her face again. He threw up his hands, turned around, went back into his office, called his assistant, and said, *Get this woman off my back. I cannot take any more of this. Fix her problem. Get her out of my life.*

The Point

What is the point of the parable? Sometimes we can miss the message of an object lesson. Do you recall the story about the temperance lecture in elementary school? The teacher had a glass of whiskey on her desk. To show how destructive whiskey is, she dropped a worm into the glass. Immediately

She kept coming to him.

the worm was zapped, shrivelled, and destroyed. "Now, what is the moral?" she asked. "What have you learned from this demonstration?" A little boy quickly shot up his hand and said, "If you have worms, you should drink whiskey." Well, he should have seen that if you drink whiskey, you are the worm; but he missed the point.

Why did Jesus tell this parable? What is the point? Was Jesus' point that badgering, pestering, and nagging pays off? Some would agree with that. Some people operate that way in their families. They badger and pester and nag until they get what they want. I did that as a child. About my tenth year, all my dad heard from me two months before Christmas was, "I want a B-B gun." The first thing at breakfast I would say, "I want a B-B gun." Every time possible during the day I would beg, "I want a B-B gun." At night I knelt to say my prayers, "Now I lay me down to sleep, I pray the Lord my soul to keep and if I die before I wake, I want a B-B gun." Guess what? It worked! At Christmas I got a Daisy Red Rider Lever Action B-B rifle.

Application Question:
What have you been "pestering" God about lately?

Is that is what the parable teaches? It pays to badger? that if you want something, nag, nag, nag until you get it? So all of us are like that woman, right? Are we insignificant, powerless, helpless? Is our only hope to badger, pester, and nag God until our prayers are answered?

If the point is that we are to pester God, it follows then, that God is like that judge. Right? If we are going to get His attention and get anything from Him, we are going to have to badger, pester, and nag Him day and night. Right?

You are not like that helpless, impoverished, unloved woman. God certainly is not like that brutal crook of a judge who cared about no one but himself.

Wrong! Wrong! Wrong! As some young people would say, "Not!" You are *not* like that helpless, impoverished, unloved woman. God certainly is *not* like that brutal crook of a judge who cared about no one but himself.

If an unjust judge can be made willing to grant a petition, how much more willing is a just God to hear and answer the prayers of people He calls chosen ones.

God Is Not Like That Judge

Jesus' point was this: If an unjust judge can be made willing to grant a petition, a just God is much more willing to hear and answer the prayers of "His elect," people He has chosen (Luke 18:6-8). If a widow with no resources and no influence can gain justice from an unjust judge, how much more will one chosen by God to bring into His kingdom be given a quick and loving ear?

The judge was unjust. God is totally just and fair. The judge neither feared God nor cared about people. The Heavenly Judge to whom we pray is Himself God and He loves people. The judge's words and actions discouraged any asking for help. God wants us to ask for His help. "Come to Me, all who are weary and heavy-laden, and I will give you rest. Take My yoke upon you, and learn from Me, for I am gentle and humble in heart; and you shall find rest for your souls. For My yoke is easy, and My load is light" (Matt. 11:28-30).

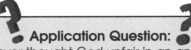

Application Question:
Have you ever thought God unfair in an answer to prayer only to find out later He really was just? Describe that time and thank Him for it.

God encourages our prayers for help, not only in word but in deed. "For God so loved the world, that He gave His only begotten Son, that whoever believes in Him should not perish, but have eternal life" (John 3:16). "But God demonstrates His own love toward us, in that while we were yet sinners, Christ died for us" (Rom. 5:8). He has shown us He truly cares for us.

Jesus came to show us that God knows what it is like *down here* and that He knows what it will take to salvage us. He came to show us what God is like *up there* and what we can expect from Him.

God is not like that judge! When Jesus Christ came to this earth, He came for several reasons. Jesus came to show us that God knows what it is like *down here* and that He knows what it will take to salvage us. He came to show us what God is like *up there* and what we can expect from Him. Everything Jesus demonstrated about God declares He is not like that judge!

God is love personified. He is the source of love. All love begins in Him and comes from Him. "Beloved, let us love one another, for love is from God; and every one who loves is born of God and knows God. The one who does not love does not know God, for God is love" (1 John 4:7-8).

We do not know what the judge lived for. His goal may have been power, wealth, fame, or any number of success substitutes to which the world calls us. We do know the passion of God. He loves people and wants to redeem people. Jesus

YOUR NOTES

(LUKE 18:1-8)

11

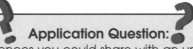
God "will bring about justice for them speedily."

declared that God sent Him to earth to seek and to save the lost (Luke 19:10).

Several summers ago I was a part of an evangelistic crusade in Dayton, Ohio. Ethel Waters, the great recording and entertainment star, sang at those meetings. One day a very bright, young, pretty, blond, and unbelieving reporter was sent to our hotel to interview those of us involved in that crusade. Her attitude was less than accepting; her spirit, less than kind. The sarcastic way she spoke let us know she was underwhelmed with her assignment.

Those of us being interviewed sat in the room where lights, cameras, and sound equipment had been assembled. Most of us had little experience with television interviews. The reporter, of course, was playing on her field. She was comfortable with the lights and the cameras, and we were not. She seemed to relish and take advantage of every opportunity to intimidate us. Several college students who had paid their own way to come and work in that crusade were almost reduced to tears.

Application Question:
What are three evidences you could share with an unbeliever that have convinced you that God loves you?

Then it was Ethel Waters's turn. As she entered the brightly lit spot where she would confront the reporter, she flashed the most dazzling smile I have ever seen. It seemed to disarm the young reporter for a second. She recovered quickly and asked in a condescending voice, "Miss Waters, what is God trying to get from us in those meetings at that football stadium?" The great singer replied, "Honey, you

do not have a thing God needs. He already has everything. He just wants to tell you He loves you, that's all." Then Miss Waters pulled from her purse a diamond ring. I have never seen that many diamonds on one ring. The diamonds formed a cross. Ethel Waters handed the ring to the reporter and let her see it was genuine and expensive. Then she named a famous actress and said, "She gave me this ring." The actress had won an academy award that year. Miss Waters continued, "Honey, she has everything you think you want, and she is miserable because she does not have Jesus."

Next it was my turn. In a very different tone the reporter said, "Mr. Pollard, would you tell us what you say to people in your meetings?" She listened quietly and attentively as I told her and those who would watch later about the love of God revealed in Jesus Christ. God is not like that judge.

Christians Are Not Like That Widow

Too many people fail to pray because they think God is like that judge—maybe not exactly like the judge, but at least too busy to hear their prayers. Perhaps even more people do not pray because they think they are not worthy of being heard by God. These are the people who see themselves as being like the widow—helpless and powerless with no influence in heavenly places.

Low self-esteem is one of the largest barriers to prayer. Like Gideon when called to be a military savior for his people, we say, *How can I do this? My family has no standing or influence, and I am the least in my family. I'm a nobody* (Judg. 6:15). God convinced Gideon that he was important to Him and His kingdom. So are you.

Application Question:
In what ways has God indicated that you are important to God's kingdom?

A psychological axiom states that you feel about yourself what you think the most important person in your life feels about you. You may be a beautiful woman or a handsome man; but if you think the most important person in your life considers you to be ugly, then you will feel ugly. You may be brilliant; but if you are convinced the most important person in your life thinks you are mentally dull, then you will feel mentally dull.

As a young man, I had no self-esteem. I hardly looked anyone in the eye. I mumbled when I talked because I thought no one was interested in what I had to say. I was sure the most important people in my life thought I was not worthy, so I did not feel worthy of anything. When I met Jesus Christ, all of that changed. For the first time I truly felt important.

> God is the President of the Universe, yet you have a private phone on His desk, and you are encouraged to call any time you want.

When Jesus Christ is the most important person in your life, you know you are loved. You know you mean so much to Him that He gave His life for you. You know that He loves you and died for you because God the Father loves you. No person or thing is more important to Him than you. He is never too busy to talk to you or to listen to you. God is the President of the Universe, yet you have a private phone on His desk, and you are encouraged to call any time you want. The Bible says you can cast all your anxiety or cares upon Him because He cares for you (1 Pet. 5:7).

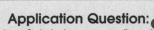

Application Question:
About what are you anxious? Jot down your "anxiety list" and in prayer give it over to Jesus.

The parable of the unjust judge is not presenting people as being like that widow or God as being like that judge. It is not teaching that prayer is badgering, pestering, or nagging.

The Power of Prayer

In the Sermon on the Mount our Lord taught Christians how to live. He told us we are the salt that preserves and saves a rotting world. He declared that we are

the only light in this dark world by which people will find their way home to the Father (Matt. 5:13-16). The rest of chapter 5 tells us how to let our light shine in such a way that people may see our good works and glorify our Father in heaven. The essential truth is that we are to out-live and out-love the rest of the world around us. That is what the world is to see. Then we are told that in order to be seen as people who out-live and out-love the world around us, there are things we do, especially in secret. In these activities we find the power to live. Prayer is one of those things (Matt. 6:5-15). God not only wants to hear from us, but He also wants to meet with us privately.

> There it is. Jesus said we are not to badger, pester, and nag as the pagans do.

Jesus told us how not to pray. "When you are praying, do not use meaningless repetition, as the Gentiles do, for they suppose that they will be heard for their many words" (Matt. 6:7). There it is. Jesus said we are not to badger, pester, and nag as the pagans do.

Do you remember when Elijah built the altar and challenged the prophets of Baal to pray down fire to consume the offering (1 Kings 18)? After the prophets of Baal prepared the offering, they "called on the name of Baal from morning until noon saying, 'O Baal, answer us.' But there was no voice and no answer" (1 Kings 18:26).

After several hours of this Elijah did a little "trash talking." He mocked them, "Call out with a loud voice, for he is a god; either he is occupied or gone aside, or is on a journey, or perhaps he is asleep and needs to be awakened" (1 Kings 18:27). They cried out louder. They cut themselves and raved all afternoon. "But there was no voice, no one answered, and no one paid attention" (1 Kings 18:29).

Then Elijah took over. He prepared a sacrifice. To emphasize his confidence in God, he had the whole altar saturated with water. Elijah then prayed a two-sentence prayer and the "fire of the Lord fell" (1 Kings 18:36-38).

Prayer is not about badgering, pestering, and nagging. Prayer is about relationship.

Prayer is not about badgering, pestering, and nagging. Prayer is about relationship. The widow in the parable had no pull, no relationship with the judge. He was not even her friend. With our Lord God it is quite different. He is much more than our friend; He is our Father.

The Importance of Prayer

When Jesus repeated a particular teaching several times, He was not being forgetful. He was emphasizing to us that which we especially need to hear and practice. Jesus told another parable that carries a similar message to that of the widow and the unjust judge (Luke 11:5-8). He asked His listeners to put themselves in this imaginary situation. You receive an unexpected guest in the middle of the night, and you have no food prepared. (The custom of hospitality in that day required a host to provide food and drink to guests.) You dash over to a friend's house, pound on the door. A sleepy voice whispers from behind the closed door, *Who is it? What do you want?* You identify yourself and ask for bread. The voice whispers again, *Go away; the family's asleep. Forget it.* You keep on knocking and asking until finally, not out of friendship but out of frustration, the man gets up and answers the request.

Does this parable sound like another recommendation for badgering, pestering, and nagging? A good friend with a full house of unexpected visitors and an empty bread box needs help. The store is closed and his neighbor is his only hope. We hear desperation knocking again. This time the desperation is not quite as severe because the man to whom the petition is made is a friend.

This story presents a situation that may portray how many of us feel about prayer. That is, God is our friend. We do not ask unless we really need something; and if we keep knocking on the door, maybe He will help us out. If you feel like that, you share an idea that is ever so accepted, ever so common, and ever so wrong.

Remember Who You Are

Who are you in this story? Are you a friend of God or are you a child of God? The friend is outside beating on the door. The children of God are inside with Him. How different in Jesus' story the response of the man would have been if his child had woke up and said, "Daddy, I'm thirsty." He would have given his best to his children. Hear Christ explain this parable. "If you then, being evil,

know how to give good gifts to your children, how much more shall your heavenly Father give the Holy Spirit to those who ask Him?" (Luke 11:13).

> When Jesus is your Savior, you are not merely a frantic friend on the outside, beating on a locked door. You are a much loved child, snuggled next to the Father.

When Jesus is your Savior, you are not merely a frantic friend on the outside, beating on a locked door. You are a much loved child, snuggled next to the Father. How much our prayers would change if we really understood that God is our Father! How much more loving, conversational, and submissively persistent our prayers would be if we could grasp the simple fact that we are much loved children of a totally loving father!

Application Question:
What are some of the terms you use to describe God? (example: all-knowing)

What is the first thing Jesus taught us to say when we pray? Father! (Matt. 6:9). Words describing God's being and attributes could fill volumes. He is all-powerful, all-knowing. He is Creator, Sustainer, Almighty God. On and on we could go and never adequately address or describe Him. Jesus said when you pray, say "Our Father."

From Roman history comes the story of an emperor in his chariot as part of a triumphant parade. The streets were lined with cheering people. Legionnaires were stationed to keep the people at a safe distance. At one point on the parade route the emperor's family sat on a platform to watch him go by in all the pride of his position.

As the emperor came near, a young boy jumped from the platform, burrowed through the crowd, and tried to dodge a legionnaire so he could run to the emperor's chariot. The soldier stopped him and said, "You cannot go out there, boy. Do you not know who is in that chariot? That is the emperor. You cannot go near him." And the little boy laughed, "He may be your emperor, but he is my father." Then he ran to his loving father's open arms. God is your Father. He loves you. He wants to listen to you.

Learning Activity 2
PRAYER
Use this page as your Bible study leader guides a season of prayer.

Adoration

Confession

Thanksgiving

Supplication

Intercession

Petition

One of the most beautiful passages of the Old Testament is that involving David and Mephibosheth. King David asked that a search be made for any surviving descendants of Saul or Jonathan (2 Sam. 9). It was discovered that a son

of Jonathan, crippled by a fall and living in poverty, was at a place called Lo-debar.

His name was Mephibosheth. David brought him out of poverty and into luxury. From the lowly hut of Machir, he was brought to the palace of the king. It was too much for him. He fell on his face and said, *What is your servant that you should show kindness to such a dead dog as I am?* And the king said in effect, *Do not call yourself a dead dog. From this day you will live in my house. You will eat at my table. From this day forward, you are a child of the king.*

This is our case. Our Lord sought us out, loved us, died for us, saved us. We come before Him saying, Lord, why do you show kindness to such a dead dog? Ears of faith can hear Him say, Do not call yourself a dead dog. From this day forward you are a child of the King. The song "A Child of the King" states:

> I once was an outcast stranger on earth,
> A sinner by choice, and an alien by birth,
> But I've been adopted, my name's written down,
> An heir to a mansion, a robe, and a crown.
> I'm a child of the King,
> A child of the King:
> With Jesus my Savior,
> I'm a child of the King.
> (Words by Harriet E. Buell, No. 555, *The Baptist Hymnal*, 1991)

And to all His children the King says, when you pray, say "Father."

Are we to pray with persistence? Is that not clearly taught in these parables in Luke? Yes, of course, it is. Our prayers are not to be offered, though, with the angry desperation of the wronged and ignored widow. We do not beat on the door until our knuckles bleed; we do not come repeatedly to God as persistent strangers or needy friends but as much loved children. We do not have to scream and yell and beat down the door. All we need to do is whisper. He is that close to us.

WHAT DOES LOVE LOOK LIKE?

■Luke 10:25-37

Part 1
Who Is My Neighbor?

We have no details about where or when this educated, religious, titled man asked his question of our Lord. Often people ask questions not to get an answer but to demonstrate their wit or to sharpen their minds on the grinding stone of argument. Sometimes they ask questions to make someone look bad, questions that simply cannot be answered well.

The man who asked Jesus how to inherit eternal life was a lawyer (Luke 10:25), a recognized expert in interpreting and applying the Scriptures. He had not come to learn from Christ. Though he addressed Jesus as "Teacher," he didn't approach the Master Teacher with a teachable attitude. The Scripture says he came to put Jesus to the test. He came to check Christ out. The implication is that he came either to make Jesus look bad or to make himself look good.

The lawyer had come up with a question for Jesus that he figured would start a theological debate. He knew Jesus had not graduated from the rabinnical school in Jerusalem. Jesus would not be aware of all the subtle twists and turns of interpretation trained scholars like himself knew. The expert was supremely confident he could impale Jesus on the horns of a dilemma. He would look good in the argument, and Christ would be discredited.

Maybe a little of all of this is meant when Scripture tells us that this doctor of biblical jurisprudence stood up to test Jesus and asked the question, "Teacher, what shall I do to inherit eternal life?" (Luke 10:25).

It's an interesting question. You don't do anything to inherit something, except wait maybe. Perhaps he was asking, *How do I know I'm in the family? How do I know I'm in line to inherit the kingdom of God?* He wasn't worried about the matter, however. If anyone was absolutely certain he would have eternal life, this man was.

No doubt the biblical expert had his argumentative ducks all lined up. Perhaps he was thinking to himself: *I'll ask my question and He'll ponder for awhile. Then if He answers in terms of faith, I'll ask, "But what about works?" If he answers with a discussion about works, well then, I'll talk about faith.*

I think this authority in the Old Testament was mentally salivating at the juicy prospect of this opportunity to parade his brilliance. So he asked his question: "What shall I do to inherit eternal life?"

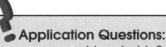

Application Questions:
In what areas are you most teachable? Least teachable?

Jesus answered him with a question: *Since you're the expert in the law, why don't you tell me what it says?* I can't tell you how disappointing an answer this must have been to the man. He was looking for stimulating and dazzling discussion, and Jesus responded merely by asking him another question. All he could do was blurt it out: *You will love the Lord your God with all your heart and soul and mind and strength and love your neighbor as yourself.*

Jesus said, *That's a good answer. Do that and you will live.*

Love always transposes into works, and there is no biblical love without faith. Likewise, there is no biblical faith without love.

Learning Activity 1
CHECK YOUR MOTIVES
Consider church or other religious activities you have been involved in during the past week. Some activities already have been listed. Add to the list in the space provided. When the study leader directs, place a check mark under the category that best describes your motivation. What was your motive? Like any other self-evaluation, this tool is helpful only if you are painfully honest with yourself.

Christian Activity	Sense of Duty	Love
Morning Worship	____	____
Sunday School	____	____
Committee Meeting	____	____
_____	____	____
_____	____	____
_____	____	____
_____	____	____
_____	____	____

Do you "do" something to inherit eternal life? ____YES ____ NO

Listen carefully to what Jesus told the man. He did not tell him that because he gave an accurate answer, he would have eternal life. The proud man of scriptural experience probably was like many of us. He had read Scripture all his life. He had memorized these words. He had quoted them, but he had never grasped the truth behind the words.

Jesus quoted those same verses when asked about the greatest commandment, explaining that these two commands sum up the entire content of God's laws and teachings in the Old Testament (Matt. 22:36-40). The problem is that no one aside from Jesus ever persistently and perfectly kept God's laws. All of us, including the pompous expert who presumed to test Jesus, have consistently broken God's laws.

A jailer in Philippi once asked Paul and Silas a question similar to that of the lawyer. He too wanted to know how to have eternal life, so he asked, "What must I do to be saved?" They replied that the way to life was to believe (place faith) in the Lord Jesus (Acts 16:30-31). He is the One God sent to make atonement for our sins, our breaking God's laws, through His selfless, loving, voluntary, sacrificial death on the cross.

We cannot enter into eternal life based on keeping God's law. Galatians 3:6-14 says the way to eternal life is and always has been the way of faith, not of keeping the law. We are saved by *grace* through *faith* that results in *works* (Eph. 2:8-10).

That being true, how are we to understand Jesus' affirming the man's answer about how to have eternal life? The command to love God with all that is within us can be understood as including faith. Ephesians 2:8-10 shows that both grace and works are involved in faith. Faith is the root of salvation and works are the fruit of salvation. Love always transposes into works, and there is no biblical love without faith. Likewise, there is no biblical faith without love. Through Luke 10:25-37, we can hear Jesus saying to us today: *Having eternal life is determined by relating to the Lord God by faith in His Son. Knowing God through Me is not about studying the doctrines of faith and love and grace and work. Knowing Me is about loving God and the people He loves. It is about relationships.*

The law expert realized he had sprung his own trap. He was like a school boy who had made up his own examination and then passed it. He had to keep this discussion going so it would look as if he were justified in quizzing Jesus. He had a quick mind; and acting as though this were his point all along, he looked bemused, winked at his friends, and asked, "And who is my neighbor?"

Application Question:

Who is *your* neighbor?

That could elicit a long morning's discussion, couldn't it? Who is my neighbor? The man probably expected Jesus to talk about the four Greek words for love, and instead our Lord simply told a story. We call it the parable of the good Samaritan.

All of us need to ask the question, Who is my neighbor? The answer is found in your heart and expressed in your world.

Our Lord took the matter out of the world of theory and discussion and put all who heard into the real world of evil, crime, pain, suffering, need, flashing red lights, sounds of gunshots, and emergency rooms. He showed us that the world desperately needs neighbors. All of us need to ask the question, Who is my neighbor? The answer is found in your heart and expressed in your world.

In our world are four kinds of people. They are found in this parable.

Learning Activity 2
WHO IS MY NEIGHBOR?

Use the following guide as you make notes during the group discussion:

1. Those Who Do Bad Things

2. Those Who Are Victims

3. Those Who Are Expected to Help But Do Not

    A.) The Priest

    B.) The Levite

4. Those Who Are Not Expected to Help But Do

YOUR NOTES

(LUKE 10:25-37)

Those Who Do Bad Things

There are those who do bad things—the crooks. Their motto is: What's yours is mine, and I'll take it. They believe what a young man told me as he was waiting on death row to be executed. He said, "My father taught me that whatever I was strong enough and smart enough to take, I had the right to take." I submit to you it is difficult for God to forgive these people. In fact, it is difficult for God to forgive sin because

> There are those who do bad things—the crooks. Their motto is: What's yours is mine, and I'll take it.

God loves people. You say, "No, preacher. If God loves people, it must be easy for Him to forgive sin." No. Sin always hurts people, and it is difficult for God to forgive that.

Application Question:
When was the last time you took an action motivated by the thought "this is my right"?

Those Who Are Victims

Another kind of person is in this story. There is one who was hurt by the people who do bad—the victim.

A newspaper told about authorities finding a little two-year-old child abandoned by his parents. He was naked and drinking from a beer bottle in a filthy home. He was a victim. Who was his neighbor?

> God's Word to us is that we are to be the kind of people who love our enemies. We will not do evil to them. We will do good to them, we will pray for them, we will help them, and we will give to them.

The evening news reported a series of murdered "women of the night." Some people responded to this with an indifferent, "Well, those women were prostitutes." Listen, God loves those women as much as He loves us. God's Word to us is that we are to be the kind of people who love our enemies. We will not do evil to them. We will do good to them, we will pray for them, we will help them, and we will give to them (Luke 6:27-36). In this world are victims who have been hurt by people who do bad things, and this breaks God's heart.

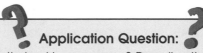

Application Question:
When were you victimized by someone? Describe the occasion:

Those Who Are Expected to Help But Do Not

Another kind of people is in this story. Sometimes in this world there are those you expect to do good things—and they do not. We read that the priest and the Levite were coming by and we say to ourselves, *Ah, help is on the way. It's going to be fine. They are going to stop and help him.* Surprise! They did not.

> Sometimes in this world there are those you expect to do good things—and they do not.

Now you understand, this is a parable. Jesus made up this story. These are not real people. If these were real people, none of us could dare say we know why they acted as they did and we know what they were about. Because these are fictional characters, we can ascribe motives to them as long as we understand this is fictional and we are speculating.

The priests not only had to come from the tribe of Levi, the tribe God set aside for religious work, but also from the lineage of Aaron. Priests were born to their priesthood. They were in charge of the sacrificial rites. If a priest touched a dead person, he was considered defiled and had to go through an expensive, lengthy rite of purification. Maybe this priest said to himself, *I don't have time to get involved with this injured man. Maybe the man is already dead.*

Or perhaps he thought, *That ditch doesn't exactly appear inviting; and besides, that guy may not even go to church. Hey, those robbers may still be around, and I've got temple money with me! The risk is too great. Surely the Lord wouldn't want me to lose His money.* Whatever his motive, the priest decided he would have nothing to do with the man. Maybe he didn't like the man's looks—after all, religious people are sometimes known by the company they avoid, right?

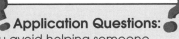

Application Questions:
When did you avoid helping someone . . .
  a. to protect your reputation?

  b. because they were not church people?

  c. because you did not want to take a risk?

  d. because you did not care?

Then came the Levite. The Levite was a descendent of Levi, but not of Aaron. The Levites were official religious functionaries as were the priests, but Levites did the more practical and mundane things around the temple.

This Levite may have been on his way to speak about brotherly love somewhere and didn't have time to stop. Perhaps he was the kind of fellow who loved programs—he didn't work much with individuals, but he loved programs. He may have been like the guy who said, "I love mankind. It's people I can't stand." Maybe he looked at that scene and said, *Wow, this will make a great illustration, and I can start a new ministry out of this. We can begin a "save people from the ditch" ministry.* His excitement was short-lived and he went on his merry way.

Application Question:
Have you ever been too busy to help someone in need because of a religious activity? If so, describe the occasion:

Those Who Are Not Expected to Help But Do

Then came a Samaritan—the man you would not expect to help. He is like the many people in this world you meet who

Then came a Samaritan—the man you would not expect to help.

"He felt compassion, and came to him, and bandaged up his wounds."

do good when you don't expect them to.

Jesus really put a zinger in this story when he identified the man who helped as being a Samaritan. You know about the relationship of Samaria and Judea. After the death of Solomon, Rehoboam foolishly led the ten tribes, the Northern Kingdom, to separate from the Southern Kingdom. They became known in history as Israel, Ephraim, and later Samaria. In 722 B.C. Samaria fell to the Assyrians, and its leading citizens were dispersed throughout the Assyrian Empire while many non-Jewish people were brought in. This led to intermarriages. The resulting population was called "half-breed" by the people of Judea. They would not let Samaritans participate in the rebuilding of the temple in Jerusalem. The Samaritans built their own temple on Mount Gerizim, and the people from Judea attacked and destroyed that temple. So great was the hostility between Jews and Samaritans that Jesus' opponents could think of nothing worse to call him than "a Samaritan" and demon possessed (John 8:48). To Jesus' audience, *good Samaritan* was an oxymoron—the words *good* and *Samaritan* did not go together.

The Samaritan gave what he had. He gave his time. He gave his substance. He gave the use of his donkey. He gave his money. He probably tore his own clothes to have bandages for binding the man's wounds. Less likely to help than anyone in the story except the crooks was the man who became the neighbor.

I once heard about a testimony given in a Wednesday evening service. A single parent with a teenage son living at home stood and said: "The other day I was

preparing a pie at home and the phone rang. It was a nurse from school who said, 'Your son has fever. Would you please come pick him up and take him home?'"

The mother explained that she put the pie in the oven because the school was but a few minutes away. When she arrived at the school, the nurse said the son's fever was high and that she should take him immediately to a doctor. The mother drove to the clinic and waited until the doctor could see her son. The doctor told her to put the boy to bed. He handed her a prescription and said to begin giving the medicine right away.

 Application Question:

Have you ever been helped by a person you least expected to help you? Describe the situation:

SARAH FOSTER

She took her son home and drove to the mall drugstore. When she came out with the medicine, she realized she had locked her keys in the car. Frantic, she called her son and told what she had done. Barely able to speak, he said, "Mother, get a wire coat hanger." Then he hung up. Eventually, she found one in the mall. Going out to the car, she realized she didn't know what to do with it.

She said, "I began to cry and then I began to pray. I said, 'Dear Lord, my boy is home sick with a fever and I have some medicine I need to give him; a pie is in the oven and I'm afraid it's going to burn up. Lord, I have locked my keys in my car. I've got this wire coat hanger I don't know what to do with. Would you please send someone to help?'"

At that moment, an old battered car parked right in front of her. A tough-looking boy got out, and she put that coat hanger in front of his face and said, "Young man, do you know how to get into a locked car with a coat hanger?"

They walked to her car and in no time he had the door unlocked. The distraught woman hugged him and said, "You are a good boy. You must be a Christian." He looked at her and said, "No ma'am. I'm not a Christian and I'm not a good boy. I just got out of prison yesterday." She hugged him again and said, "Bless God. He sent me a professional!"

There are those we do not expect to help who surprise us.

> A neighbor is anyone you see whose needs you can help meet.

Who Is a Neighbor?

The least likely helper became the neighbor. A neighbor is anyone you see whose needs you can help meet. These "neighbors" may not be people like you. They may not be people you would like. You may have no indication that they would be a neighbor to you, but God wants His people in this world to be neighbors to everyone who needs a neighbor.

What could be more important than helping other people out of an overflowing love for God? When you and I ask Jesus, How do I live a life that befits a child of God? He answers, You will love the Lord your God with all your heart, with all your soul, with all your mind, and with all your strength; and you will love your neighbor as yourself. And when you ask, Who is my neighbor? He will say: Your neighbor is anyone you see whose needs I have put you in a position to meet.

Part 2
Whose Neighbor Am I?

Who is my neighbor? is a good question; but Jesus had an even better question in mind for the lawyer. He set him up for it by telling him the story about the good Samaritan. Then Jesus asked, "Which of these three do you think proved to be a neighbor to the man who fell into the robbers' hands?" Jesus was saying, *The question is not Who is your neighbor? Rather, it is To whom should you be a neighbor? Whose neighbor are you?*

That is the question for you and me. I would like to know more about many things in this story, wouldn't you? As you picture the events happening, wouldn't you like to know how deep the ditch was? How hard was it to get that man out of it? Was the victim a big man? Was he heavy? Was it difficult to get him on the donkey? Was the donkey able to carry such a load? Was the donkey old? young? strong? weak? Who was the Samaritan? What was his business? How old was he?

When Should We Be a Neighbor?

How old do you have to be to go on God's "ditch patrol"? When do you begin doing ditch patrol for the glory of God? When are you too old for ditch patrol? When does ditch patrol end?

Does the idea of being on ditch patrol sound above your ability? I heard about a little girl whose desk mate in the first grade had lost her mother to a terrible disease. The grieving daughter came back to school after the funeral. When her friend and desk mate came home from school, her mother asked, "Your desk mate came back today, didn't she?"

The girl said, "Yes."

"Well, what did she do?" the mother asked.

She said, "Mother, it was a terrible day for her. She put her head down on her desk and cried."

The mother then asked, "Well, honey, what did you do?"

She said, "I put my head down on my desk and cried with her."

That's being on ditch patrol. Who cannot do that? That's how God wants us to react to the hurting people in this world. When do you become exempt from that? When do you get over that? When do you stop being on ditch patrol?

I've observed in our society nowadays that people are living more years, but many of them are not getting old. Such people just stay young. They keep doing better and better and stay younger and younger. Perhaps it's because they stay active. Have you noticed?

I suppose you keep being on ditch patrol as long as you can stay active—as long as you can do it. Our Lord has put us here for some reason. I think this parable tells us we are here to love Him with all our hearts and souls and minds and strength and to love our neighbors as ourselves. The parable of the good Samaritan shows us what love looks like. Loving our neighbor as ourselves looks like helping anyone we can. Our neighbor is anyone we see whose need we can meet. The questions we must confront every day are: To whom will I be a neighbor? For whom am I responsible? How far am I willing to go to be a neighbor? Whose neighbor am I?

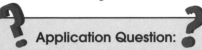

Application Question:
Who are some people you have cared for in some way this week?

What Makes You a Neighbor?

Did you ever wonder why the Samaritan was concerned when others weren't? How could wonderfully respectable, religious people pass by on the other side? How could this man about whom we know so very little—except that he was not racially acceptable to the people hearing the story—be the one to help? What made him a neighbor? Why did he stop? What caused him to do this?

One line in our text gives the answer: "When he saw him, he felt compassion" (Luke 10:33). He cared. He had a heart for caring. Where do you get a heart like that? Our natural heart is not like that. We are not born that way. It's not the way we are. The Bible explains that when it says "for all have sinned and fall short of the glory of God" (Rom. 3:23). "All of us like sheep have gone astray, each of us has turned to his own way" (Isa. 53:6). The Bible declares that our hearts are selfish. Our tendency is to look out for ourselves, not for others. Our hearts are exceedingly deceitful and wicked (Jer. 17:9).

We need God to come and give us a new heart.

We need a heart transplant. We need God to come and give us new hearts. Ezekiel asserted that God will give you a new heart and a new spirit (Ezek. 11:19). The apostle Paul, initially hatchet man for the religious mafia, became one of the greatest Christians—one of the sweetest, most loving ditch-patrol people you ever saw. What happened? Paul explained it like this: "If any man is in Christ, he is a new creature" (2 Cor. 5:17).

God gives you a heart transplant when you come to Him in Christ. Only those who have received that new heart will see and care about the people in the ditch. Those who have a new heart can begin to say, *I do love the Lord my God with all my heart and soul and mind and strength and I'll love my neighbor as myself.* You get that kind of heart from God through Jesus Christ. He gives you that new heart.

Will You Be a Neighbor?

Do you see them? Do you see the people in the ditches all around you? Do you see that man whose wife has been stolen by another man and whose life is crushed? His heart is broken and he's lying in that ditch. Do you see that woman who lost her husband to some terrible disease and the light of her life is gone? Do you see teenagers facing what this pitiful society is throwing at them?

Do you see the people lying in the ditch near you? Do you see the little child? A sweet, helpless little child who will never have a chance for joy, who will never have the chance for a happy childhood because he has selfish and abusive parents—the plight of too many children. People all around us are lying in life's ditches, beaten, left there half dead, ignored by so many of us who call ourselves religious. Do you see them?

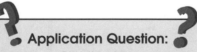

Application Question:
What things cause a Christian to become hardened?

Unfortunately, Christians can become hardened. I'm not saying we can lose our salvation, but we can become hard-hearted. David did. You recall how David became so hardened that he committed adultery and then committed murder to cover it up (2 Sam. 11—12). He was a man after God's own heart, but he let his heart become calloused. He became like the robbers when he took a man's wife and life. He was like the priest and Levite when he tried to pretend his sins of adultery and murder did not matter. He was not helping victims—he was making victims. When he came to himself with the help of the prophet Nathan, David prayed, *Oh, God, give me a new heart. Renew a right spirit within me. Clean up my heart* (Ps. 51:10).

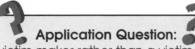

Application Question:
Have you been a victim-maker rather than a victim-helper in some ways? List here actions you need to take toward God and other specific individuals:

This world can be made better by people on ditch patrol. People who can see a need, who can see the hopeless and helpless, and who are unselfishly willing to do something for them can change the world.

This world can be made better by people on ditch patrol.

Is This What Love Looks Like?

Many of us know the story of Helen Keller. Before she was two years old, she was stricken with a disease that left her blind, mute, and deaf. She was in a deep, dark ditch with no communication with any other human being. She received no sights or sounds from the world around her. What deeper and darker ditch could one experience?

Application Question:
What keeps you from seeing needs around you?

Years before Helen Keller was born, a girl called Little Annie was committed to a mental institution near Boston. In those days no help was available for people as insane as Little Annie apparently was. So they put her in "the dungeon," the cellar of the building. They fed her and clothed her and kept her in a cage down in the dungeon.

YOUR
NOTES
(LUKE 10:25-37)

A sweet elderly nurse thought all God's creatures needed love and respect and help. This nurse sat by Little Annie in the cage every day at lunch and talked to her. At times Little Annie was violent. Other times she seemed not to recognize anyone and was unaware of what went on around her. The nurse brought some brownies and left it by Annie's cage. The next day the brownies were gone. She began to bring brownies every day she came. She worked with Annie, and soon Annie began to respond.

Annie was taken up to where patients were given treatment and care. In a few years Annie was told she could go home. Annie decided, however, that the institution meant so much to her she would stay there and help others. She trained to be a nurse.

Helen Keller received an award presented by the Queen of England, Queen Victoria, for giving service and inspiration to many in this world. Helen Keller had become one of the most sensitive, caring, ministering people the world has known. When asked to make some remarks, she said, "Had it not been for my nurse, Anne Sullivan, no one would ever have heard of me. She is the one who loved me, who prayed for me, who witnessed to me, who shared Christ with me. She is the one who taught me that I was loved and that I could be loving. She is the one who taught me how to make sounds and to speak. She gave her life helping me have this ministry."

Without Anne Sullivan you never would have heard of Helen Keller. Of course, Anne Sullivan was Little Annie. Someone else went into her ditch, refused to give up on her, and helped her. Then Anne Sullivan went into Helen Keller's ditch and helped her—and the world was made better because of it.

You can go into people's ditches of distress and despair to minister to them in many ways. I've often wondered about the man in the ditch in Jesus' story. I've wondered what the rest of his life was like. Did he remember the cruelty of the robbers and, therefore, become bitter and angry for the rest of his life? Or did he remember the kindness of the good Samaritan and spend the rest of his life trying to be like him?

Who Is Responsible?

Are you ready to get more involved in God's ditch patrol? Or are you leaving it up to others?

A church in a rural area had only one Sunday School department. All the boys and girls and men and women met together for the general assembly. Each class took turns leading the opening assembly. One Sunday the children's department presented a pantomime of the story of the good Samaritan.

The best reader in class, Olga, stood up to read the part about a man on his way from Jerusalem to Jericho who fell among thieves, was beaten, robbed and left half dead. Mark, who had been sitting on the front row, got up, walked across the stage and the "thieves" who had been waiting behind the piano and the desk jumped out and grabbed him. They cleaned his spark plugs, gave him a general overhaul, and left him half dead right there on the stage.

Application Question:

When is the last time you found yourself saying to yourself, "It is somebody else's job"?

Write a one-sentence prayer asking God's forgiveness for any specific failings to be on ditch patrol:

Olga read some more about the priest who passed by on the other side. With dramatic unconcern the "priest" pulled his robes around himself and walked by, having nothing to do with the injured man. More Scripture was read and the "Levite" came by and did the same thing, just ignored the man and walked on.

Then Olga read about the Samaritan who saw the man and cared and helped him. Everyone anticipated the action on the stage, but nothing happened. A small boy on the front row punched his friend and said, "That's you."

His friend said, "No, it's not! She told us last Sunday you were supposed to be the good Samaritan."

And the friend said, "She did not! She said *you* were supposed to."

"No, she didn't!"

While the boys argued, that fellow just lay up on the stage and died. I wonder how many of us think God told somebody else to be the good Samaritan? I wonder how many of us think that somebody else is supposed to be seeing those people in the ditch and doing something about it? I wonder—Who's your neighbor? Whose neighbor are you?

CHAPTER

WHAT IS A SECURE INVESTMENT?

■Luke 12:13-31

According to Luke 12:1, thousands of people were packed around Jesus; and one man shoved his way through the crowd and shouted, *Lord, I have a favor to ask. Make my brother divide the inheritance.* A convincing proof of the divine wisdom of our Lord is that He did not get involved in that. Nothing divides a family more quickly than fussing over who gets what.

The Lie That Deceives Multitudes

Christ said in effect, *That is not my business, but you are my business; and I must warn you against greed.*

What a timely warning! Greed does not tell us the truth; it lies to us. It tells us that "life" consists in the abundance of our possessions. We had better hang around that line a while. We live a little too close to the idea that greed is good. One of Wall Street's most successful men was convicted and imprisoned. He had said, "Greed is wonderful. Greed is the secret of my success."

Have we bought greed's lie that life consists in the abundance of things owned? People are made in the image of God. Genesis 1—2 states clearly that human life is the greatest of all God's creation. Yet what do we mean when we ask questions like, How much is he or she worth? Why do we answer only in terms of dollars? When we talk of standards of living, why does the conversation have nothing to do with *standards* or *living*? Have we believed the lie that life consists in the abundance of things possessed? Christ would have us stand guard over our minds at this point. Do not allow into your mind the idea that what you have is what you are.

Application Question:

How do you measure the worth of others?

Obviously we cannot leave the matter there. Serious followers of Christ have too many unanswered questions about what gives meaning to life. If life is not in things possessed, where is it? Is being successful wrong? Is being unsuccessful spiritual? What about all those friends of Jesus who seemed to be more than well off? What about all the good that can be done with wealth?

The Farm That Owned a Fool

To expose greed's lies, Jesus told a story about a successful farmer. Evidently, he was hardworking and knew how to farm. Over a particular year the rains had come softly and at the right time. The winds were gentle and the crops were fantastic. As the farmer surveyed the abundance growing from his ground, he began to see its implication. *This is going to be a good year,* he said to himself. Then he

"You have many goods laid up for many years to come."

began to plan his future, *I have worked hard all these years to build up this farm. Now this is the payoff. I will build bigger barns, silos, and granaries; and in them I will store this vast wealth. I will be able to slack off, to slow down, to eat, drink, and enjoy life.* Eleven times in three verses we read the pronouns, "I" and "my" (12:17-19).

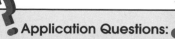

Application Questions:
How can you show gratitude for success to the Lord? to employees/employer/coworkers? to the community?

In all the farmer's plans of what he would do with his bountiful economic boon, we read not one word about the tithe to the Lord who gave him life, wisdom, and strength. He expressed no gratitude to the One who brought the rains to water the crops, the winds to cross-fertilize the crops, or the sunshine to ripen the crops. No mention is made of rewarding the good people who worked with him, who plowed, planted, and cultivated the crops. We see no sign of a sense of social obligation to better the community in which he lived. The only beneficiary in his mind and plan was himself. *I have got it made. Now life can be easy. I will dedicate the rest of my life to finding pleasure and avoiding pain.*

The Lord God who wanted so much to be his Savior is forced to come as his Judge.

I picture the farmer having those thoughts late at night while sketching plans for the new barn. Suddenly he hears a noise. The doors are locked, but Someone is in the room with him—Someone strange and unfamiliar and frightening. He has ignored the Lord God all his life. Now he is experiencing that inevitable meeting we all will have. He would not seek God. He would not respond to all those urges he felt when God sought him. The Lord God who wanted so much to be his Savior is forced to come as his Judge. The loving Lord whose greatest desire was to bring him love and peace must now administer judgment and punishment.

What did God call this man who was successful, visionary, hardworking, and perhaps the most powerful man in his community? "Fool!" He called the man a fool. *You Fool! You*

Learning Activity 1
WHAT OWNS YOU?

Personalize the parable by answering the following questions.

(1) For farming to be successful, the farmer had to depend on many resources beyond his control. On what resources beyond your control do you depend for success in your business and family life?

(2) The farmer refused to express appropriate appreciation for any of these resources. How can you appropriately show appreciation for these resources?

To whom should you show your appreciation?

(3) God and the farmer had quite different perspectives on the farmer's situation. How do you think God would view your business and/or money management?

(4) The farmer relied totally on earthly investments for his future security. On what are you relying?

have spent your life, your wit, and your energy planning for a future you do not have. Does it strike you as ungodly for God to call this respectable, successful man a fool? It is not. God simply named him for what he was.

God called the farmer a fool. The next morning his wife found his body on the floor of the den by the large table where he had been sketching the drawing for the barn. In big bold letters over the sketching she saw written, "Inscribe on my tombstone 'Here lies a fool.'"

What is a fool? What kind of man did God Himself call a fool? We are not told he was dishonest or immoral, but the story does tell us he was a thankless man,

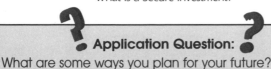

Application Question:
What are some ways you plan for your future?

not given to gratitude. He was foolish because he believed greed's lie. He invested in a future he did not have and refused to invest in a future he could have had. In the Sermon on the Mount Jesus addressed the topic of wise and secure investing.

> He invested in a future he did not have and refused to invest in a future he could have had.

Making Wise, Secure Investments (Matt. 6:19-24)

We often overlook this momentous fact about Christ: He did not come to impose a burden on people; He came to lift people's burdens. He did not come to take away the joy of life; He came to instill joy into life. Too many times, in this age of guided missiles and misguided people, Christ has been taken to be a cosmic killjoy, a sort of resident policeman who raps our knuckles when we appear to be having fun. Before you fall for this satanic slander, let me remind you that Christ said, "I came that they might have life, and might have it abundantly" (John 10:10).

> Christ . . . did not come to impose a burden on people; He came to lift people's burdens. He did not come to take away the joy of life; He came to instill joy into life.

In the Sermon on the Mount (Matt. 5—7), Christ summed up what it means to live the Christian life. The opening word, the keynote of this magnificent charter of the kingdom of God, is the word "blessed." "Blessed" means happy. Do you see it? Christ has always said it, thousands have discovered it—the way of Christ is the blessed way, the happy way.

Beginning in Matthew 6:19, Jesus indicated that to experience the abundant life, we need to know how to deal with material things. Both having money and lacking enough money have caused more heartbreak than perhaps any other thing. This is so great an obstacle to the blessed life that a large percentage of all Christ had to say dealt with some aspect of the subject.

Every Christian is a citizen of two worlds, and those worlds are so different! In our best moments we know that both worlds, then and now, are to be committed to God—and that Christian consistency commands commitment of every part of our lives.

So there comes a time when a follower of Christ must ask, How do I feel about things? If I love Christ, how do I feel about my car? If He is my Master, how do I handle my money? Does this mean I have to hate things and spurn them?

Application Questions:
Have you ever struggled with questions like these: How do I feel about things? If I love Christ, how do I feel about my car? If He is my Master, how do I handle my money? Does this mean I have to hate things and spurn them? What conclusions have you reached?

These are not questions with easy, pat, glib answers. We know we are made in God's image, thus we are spiritual. Also, we are aware of being made of earth to live on earth, so we are material. How do you reconcile being made of the dust and being made in the image of Deity? How can we cope with being both material and spiritual? Each Christian struggles with the question, How in heaven's name do I treat earth's things?

So in His sermon on the happy way of abundant life, Jesus spoke to us about wise and secure investing. He talked specifically of the passion for possession, the principles of possessing, and the position of priority.

The Passion for Possession
We have to keep reminding ourselves that we are creatures made by God. This means that basically we are as God made us. Now don't misunderstand. I am not saying we are as God meant us to be. We are not, because everyone's life has been twisted by sin. Here is what I am saying: we have God-given instincts, but sin has perverted these drives and desires.

For instance, consider one of the major cracks in our culture today—the inordinate, unnatural obsession with sex. This is simply a case where Satan has been allowed to take a God-given desire and bend it all out of proportion until it is perverted.

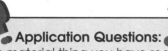

Application Questions:
What is some material thing you have recently found yourself really wanting?

Why do you think you desire it so?

Or take the matter of gambling, a foolish, often addictive way Satan erodes the character. We have this instinct for enterprise, the perversion of which is to gamble. God wants us to place our lives in His hands by faith, a great risk, if you please, in order that we may fulfill this instinct for enterprise, this desire for real adventure.

When we have God in our hearts, we do not need demeaning crutches.

Then there are alcohol and other drugs. Everyone has a hunger in the heart that merely living out days in animal-like fashion cannot fulfill. This is the hunger only God can satisfy. Satan perverts this desire and leads many misguided souls to seek refuge in a bottle, a pill, or needle, only to find greater distress. The Bible states, "Do not get drunk with wine, for that is dissipation, but be filled with the Spirit" (Eph. 5:18). When we have God in our hearts, we do not need demeaning crutches.

Just as every source of energy and power must be bridled and guided, even so must be this desire to have.

Just as every other drive and desire is God-given—though sin-perverted—even so is the passion for possession. We read Christ's words, "Do not lay up for yourselves treasures upon earth," and tend to forget that He also said, "But lay up for yourselves treasures" (Matt. 6:19-20). It is not the passion that is wrong, but its perversion. Here then we see what Christ was getting at—passion for possession without principle is perilous. Just as every source of energy and power must be bridled and guided, even so must be this desire to have. Our loving Lord would say to us, *I made you with a passion to possess. I want you to have; I want you to possess; but I want you to possess the best.*

The Principles for Possessing

In Matthew 6:19-21 Christ presented Christian principles of possessing. The first is this: **Temporary holdings do not constitute real riches.**

All our material possessions are temporarily in our hands. Sooner or later we will leave them behind.

I heard a man from Latvia tell what happened when communists took over his country. He was a member of a wealthy family whose chief holding was a giant city department store. "The day the communists came," he said, "we were able to take out of the store only the clothes we were wearing. We left everything we owned in Latvia and fled for our freedom." All our material possessions are temporarily in our hands. Sooner or later we will leave them behind.

Our Lord is saying to us through these words in Matthew, *Because I love you, I do not want you to spend your short but valuable lives piling up temporary treasure. Haven't you lived long enough to observe that just about the time a person says, "I've got it made," time runs out on him or her? Don't you know that earth's treasures are always being eaten by moths of depreciation, wasted by the rust of inflation, and stolen by the thousand and one varieties of thieves that inhabit this earth?*

Why don't we listen to Christ when He asks this pertinent question, "For what will a man be profited, if he gains the whole world, and forfeits his soul?" (Matt 16:26).

Make your fortune, but store it in a place where you can keep it—invest it in the kingdom of God.

Here is the second principle: **Eternal investment is wisest.** "But lay up for yourselves treasures in heaven" (Matt. 6:20). God wants us to possess; He wants us to have, but He wants us to have the best. If you make your fortune on earth, you have made a fortune and stored it in a place where you cannot hold it. Make your fortune, but store it in a place where you can keep it—invest it in the kingdom of God and let it draw interest, compounded through eternity.

Investments in heaven may well include all we take with us into eternity—all our Christian growth and service. In this context, though, Christ was talking about material wealth. He was not speaking of prayers you store up in heaven or work you do for which you shall be rewarded. Here He was speaking of money.

> Your treasure itself is not so important, but what it does to your heart is supremely important.

Here is the third principle: **We always look after our investments.** "For where your treasure is, there will your heart be also" (Matt. 6:21). Your treasure itself is not so important, but what it does to your heart is supremely important. This is why the love of money is called "a root of all sorts of evil" (1 Tim. 6:10). Passion for possessions can pull you down to a low level and fill your life with a frustration of temporariness. Your every desire, every joy, and every mood is then directly related to the condition of the market and your bank account. If you properly invest in heaven, though, you can anchor your soul, fix your attention on the eternal, and keep your heart in the condition God wants it to be—and you will find true happiness.

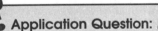

Application Question:
When has your mood been affected by material or financial matters?

Christ brought to us the urgency of having a right relationship to the material by discussing two kinds of vision (Matt. 6:22-23). He spoke of a "clear" eye and a "bad" eye. We must see clearly to have a true view. A clear eye means that vision is unified; both eyes are singularly focused. The word translated "bad" means *sick*. An eye that doesn't work properly is out of order. If your view of material goods is out of order, then your whole body is full of darkness. You are seeking abundant life in the wrong arena, and you won't find it. People aware that their vision is impaired walk with caution to make sure they do not fall into the ditch. If one has faulty vision and mistakes the ditch for the road and the road for the ditch, then disaster is certain.

> If your view of material goods is out of order, then your whole body is full of darkness.

Far, far too many are suffering from a view of life that is completely out of order. One Christian has asserted that perhaps the most ironical commentary on our civilization is that we live on earth as though this were heaven and regard heaven as though it were earth. We treat time as eternity and view eternity as though it were the brief digit of time.

Do not be in the habit of laying up treasures on earth because there your heart will be. You must look after your investments—that is the lesson. You will keep your eye on your treasure, and happy is the day when the treasure pulls the eye into the gaze of heaven.

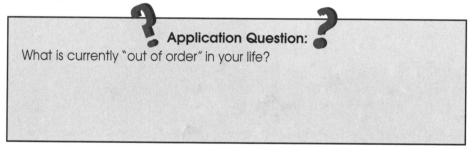

Application Question:
What is currently "out of order" in your life?

The Position of Priority

The principles of possessing are needful because God demands the position of priority. "No one can serve two masters; . . . You cannot serve God and mammon" (Matt. 6:24).

> We have this passion to possess. . . .We will do with it what we do with any passion. We will worship with it.

Here is the deepest and most profound element in the principles of possessing. We have this passion to possess. What will we do with it? We will do with it what we do with any passion. We will worship with it. We may worship God with

it—we may worship mammon (money) with it. We cannot, however, worship both God and money. This is the whole point.

No one can become the slave of earthly treasure and worship it without thereby proving oneself a traitor to God. Jesus' parable of the rich fool shows that. The opposite is also true. No one can be a bond servant of God, worshiping Him with all the heart, and be enslaved by money.

Segregation indeed can be an ugly word. There is a kind of segregation more sinful than racial segregation. It is an approach to life that supposes our days to be partitioned, like the pigeonholes in an old-fashioned rolltop desk. People who have adopted this approach think religion and business are completely different and unrelated matters. They are offended at the idea that their faith may have something to say about how they get and use their income. They assume money management is not included in God's area of operation. They mentally lock God in the church building and press Him into the Bible like some faded rose petal.

Perhaps the rich fool operated that way. Do you? If so, it is time for you to know that God is the Lord of the warehouse as well as the worship service. It is time for you to search a seldom dusted corner of God's Word in Deuteronomy 8:18 and hear loudly and clearly, "You shall remember the Lord your God, for it is He who is giving you power to make wealth."

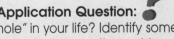

Application Question:
Do you "pigeonhole" in your life? Identify some areas of life that you have made it a practice not to mix with Christianity.

Jesus did not ask every wealthy person He met to sell everything and give the proceeds to the poor. When He did ask a man to do that, it was apparent this man thought he owned his things when his things really owned him. Our Lord was simply trying to free him from a cruel master (see Luke 18:18-25).

"Do you 'pigeonhole' in your life?"

A close study of Jesus' teachings causes us to think many churches have been presenting the wrong primary reasons for giving. We often have appealed for giving because of the ministries that are supported by the money, and this is important. So many life-and-death ministries are involved! An even more significant concern should be ourselves as we face the constant danger that our things may become our god. As you give part of your time, your toil, and yourself, which is all money is, you are avoiding this danger.

A radiantly happy woman was asked the secret of her success in life. She answered, "I have never allowed the dollar bill to get bigger than my God."

Application Question:

Why do you give (or not give) to your church?

The Old Testament commands, "Honor the Lord from your wealth" (Prov. 3:9). The New Testament tells us how to honor the Lord with our money. Concerning a plan for giving, we read, "On the first day of every week let each one of you put aside and save, as he may prosper" (1 Cor. 16:2). This is giving, born not of whim or of impulse, but of an orderly plan sustained by love for the Lord who gives us the power to get wealth.

Such giving reflects a determination that money will be our servant, not our god. "No man can serve two masters." You cannot serve God and money.

The rich farmer was a fool because he did not understand eternal investments. He was a fool because he was not prepared to die. Is the basis of your security wise or foolish? What changes do you need to make to demonstrate that your basis of security is wise?

The Preparation That All Must Make

Did you know that the ratio of living to dying is one to one? One out of every one person dies. What a foolish thing not to be prepared for something you know will happen! How chilling are the words, "But God said to him, 'You fool! This very night your soul is required of you'" (Luke 12:20).

Evangelist D. L. Moody said that he made his greatest mistake on October 8, 1871. On that night in Chicago, he addressed one of the largest crowds of his career. His message was about the Lord's trial and was based on Pilate's question, "What then shall I do with Jesus?" (Matt. 27:22).

As Moody concluded, he said, "I wish you would seriously consider this subject, for next Sunday we will speak about the cross, and at that time I'll inquire, 'What will YOU do with Jesus?'" Ira Sanky began to sing the closing hymn which includes the lines, "Today the Savior calls; for refuge fly. The storm of justice falls, and death is nigh."

Sanky never finished the hymn; it was interrupted by the rush and roar of fire engines on the street outside. That was the night of the great Chicago fire. The next day, Chicago lay in ashes. "I have never since dared," said Moody, "to give an audience a week to think about their salvation."[1]

Post Script—The Farmer Who Owned a Farm

Have you ever wondered what Jesus would have said had the man in the crowd shouted out a different question? What if instead of saying, "Tell my brother to divide the family inheritance with me," he had said, "Master, teach me how to share the inheritance with my brother. What is the best and right way to do that?" "Well, that is not a question for Me to decide," Jesus may have answered. "But I congratulate you for understanding the deceitful wickedness of greed. How wise you are to know that life does not consist in the abundance of things possessed. You are to be congratulated for not letting life's furniture make a fool of you."

Then Jesus may have told a story about a farmer who owned a farm, not about a farm that owned the farmer. The farmer looked at those lush, waving acres of grain, a bumper

Learning Activity 2
IN WHAT DO YOU INVEST?

Place a check mark beside each item in which you find personal security.

____ Occupational income

____ Matthew 6:33

____ Real estate/house

____ Stocks/bonds/other financial investments

____ 401k

____ Pension plan

____ Social Security

____ Malachi 3:10

____ Anticipated inheritance from a relative

____ 2 Corinthians 9:6-8

____ Professional standing

____ Social standing

____ Proverbs 3:9-10

crop the like of which had never before been seen in that whole countryside. Then he looked to heaven and said, "Gracious Lord, how good you are. I praise you and I thank you." Later in his den, he sat at a big desk. He sketched a drawing of the new barn. Then on another sheet he carefully printed a list:

1. The tithe and gratitude to God
2. A generous bonus for the workers
3. Social Responsibilities—
 • New equipment for community park playground
 • School clothes for Bobby Green (Hudspeth's foster child)
 • Roof and window repair for widows—Joy Able, Mandy Phillips
 • Bike for Kusum Singh
 • Soon he became aware of a Presence in the room. It was a warm, loving, familiar presence he sensed. In times of worship, both public and private, he had experienced hints of that Presence; but now he felt it more than ever before. It was his beloved Heavenly Father, his Partner, his Strength and Savior. The farmer felt no fear. This was no stranger. This loving Father said, "You have done well. Now it is time for the next step. You have done well with the opportunities, abilities, mind, and help I have given you. You have been honest and fair and generous. You are a successful man. All the investments you have made in My kingdom have been deposited under your name. They are accruing interest daily, compounded throughout eternity. You are wise. You are rich toward God."

When his wife found his body on the floor the next morning, she saw that across the plans for the barn, he had written, "Inscribe my tombstone, 'For me to live is Christ, and to die is gain.'"

---

[1]Paul Lee Tan, *Encyclopedia of 7,000 Illustrations: Signs of the Times* (Rockville, Maryland: Assurance Publishers, 1979), 1220-1221. Used by permission.

8

How Does Humility Fit with Self-Esteem?

Scripture Verses

- Luke 14:7-11; 18:9-14

Confusion?

How do you understand the terms *humility* and *self-esteem?* Most people today agree that we all need to have a healthy view of ourselves in order to function well and to relate appropriately to others. After all, Jesus said that we are to love others as we love ourselves (Matt. 22:39), so we need to feel good about ourselves, right?

At the same time, Jesus taught that we are to humble ourselves. Secular people are highly in favor of self-esteem, but many of them are not so sure about humility. Even some Christians wonder how the two fit together. Are we supposed to feel good or bad about ourselves?

The confusion is rooted in false ideas about both self-esteem and humility. Self-esteem often is confused with pride, with thinking of ourselves more highly than we ought to think (Rom. 12:3), of thinking ourselves superior to others. Humility is confused with low self-esteem, of having no confidence, of feeling incompetent, inadequate, and unworthy. In other words, some view self-esteem as pompous and humility as groveling. Neither is correct.

Jesus told two parables that illustrate the importance of genuine, godly humility. Only the humble can enter the throne room of God. In God's presence we discover that we are highly loved, valued, and esteemed by God. That is the basis

for healthy, godly self-esteem. Let God speak to your heart through these two familiar parables.

Humility and Exaltation (Luke 14:7-11)

A leader of the Pharisees had invited a number of his Pharisee friends and Jesus to a meal on a Sabbath. The purpose for inviting Jesus was not social but political; "they were watching Him closely" (14:1). The Pharisees despised Jesus, viewing Him as a pretender. He simply would not conform to their preconceived ideas of religious propriety. They wanted to find something wrong with Him, something they could use to get rid of Him.

Jesus observed how the guests tried to position themselves at the places of honor around the table. Though they were His enemies, He decided to help them. He was secure enough within Himself not to permit the actions and attitudes of others to determine His own. Also, He was humble enough to reach out in love to those who wanted to do Him in. They were against Him, but He was for them. What an example of godly self-esteem and humility!

"Do not take the place of honor."

Why would Jesus give counsel about choosing a seat? What is the big deal about where people sit at a banquet? Jesus' story is a bit humorous. We can just see those men jockeying for positions of honor, looking around to see how they fit in

113

the pecking order. They could not risk being humiliated by being asked to move down to a lower seat. To find that the "chief" seat they occupied belonged to someone "chiefer" would be embarrassing. I guess it is not so funny after all when we realize that these were the spiritual leaders of their day. The Pharisees were well-known to be men of God.

This ego-serving activity was disturbing to Jesus. Why? Because these men were trying to say what some of us try to say by the clothes we wear, the homes we buy, the automobiles we drive, the positions we occupy. "Look at me. I am worth something. I am somebody. I matter. I am important." Do such status symbols make us important? Without them are we not important? Jesus made clear that we are important to Him. He wants us to have a great life. He demonstrated that our having a full and rich life is "to die for," literally.

We see then that this little parable is not just advice in banquet etiquette. Jesus was telling us that our greatness, our identity, our importance is not determined by our place at a head table.

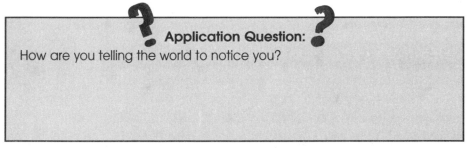

Application Question:
How are you telling the world to notice you?

The Scriptures say that wisdom comes from God. The leaders of this world are totally oblivious to this wisdom that holds the secret of life. Eyes have not seen it—it is invisible. Ears have not heard it—it is inaudible. No mind has conceived what God has prepared for those who love Him—it is incomprehensible. Yet God reveals His wisdom to those who seek it by His Spirit. The Spirit searches all things. "Even the depths of God"(1 Cor. 2:7-13). The word "depths" is a plural form of the Greek word *bathos* from which we get the word *bathysphere*. A bathysphere is a steel diving vessel that can be lowered into the ocean to explore the ocean's deepest secrets. God's Spirit wants to reveal to us God's deepest and most profound truths. Are we listening?

Many people today seem not to be listening to God. Would we be too harsh or judgmental to say that much of what we call Christianity today is shallow? It seems characterized by egotistical little people scrambling for important places to sit. This involves much church and denominational work and activity. I wonder how much of this activity is really "life" and how much of it is really "death."

We raised chickens when I was a boy. When we wanted a chicken dinner, we started with a live chicken. Today we go to a grocery store and find those poor chickens stripped, covered with goose bumps, huddling in cellophane packages. We are almost embarrassed for them.

I noticed back then that a chicken's life was a mixture of danger and pleasure. I often wondered what the chickens thought when we entered the chicken-wire prison compound where they lived. We brought them food and water on some visits, so they had to like that. On other occasions we took their eggs. When we did not bring food or water, when we did not head toward the nests to get eggs, we started for them. To me it seemed that they got a look of impending doom in their eyes.

My mother usually did the actual execution. She would grab the chicken by its head and wring its neck until its head came off. Have you ever seen what a chicken does immediately after having its head wrung off? Those headless chickens did marvelous things they had never done in a better state of health. There was a great deal of activity, but it was not life, just activity—the activity of death.

Jesus is the head of the church (Col. 1:18). I wonder what a church acts like without its head? Just because there's activity does not mean there's life. The life and wisdom of Christ does not come from activity but from the depth of the riches of God. It is imparted by the Spirit of God.

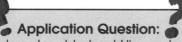

Application Question:
In Luke 14:11 Jesus taught about His way to exalted living. How did He demonstrate this verse in His life?

Religious activity may be impressive and gain recognition and even positions of honor and prestige. Recognition is OK, but be on guard against pride. Jesus said, "Everyone who exalts himself shall be humbled, and he who humbles himself shall be exalted." His purpose in telling this parable was to take us deep into ourselves and into His love. He was pointing the way to godly self-esteem, to the exalted life, to the ultimate level of living.

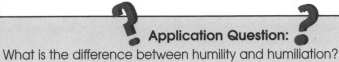

Application Question:
What is the difference between humility and humiliation?

Humility is the door to being an authentic person. Of Moses, one of history's all-time great leaders, the Holy Record says, "Moses was very humble" (Num. 12:3). However, the supreme example of humility is Jesus. In every respect a genuine and authentic person, He showed us the meaning of being truly humble. He

---

Learning Activity 1
HUMILITY

Use the following outline to take notes during the presentation on humility:

1. Humility is the first step to salvation and peace with God.

2. Humility is the secret of restoring the joy of salvation.

3. Humility is the secret of confident living.

4. Humility results in successful living.

who was over everything made Himself as nothing, taking upon Himself the very nature of a bond-servant. Then, "He humbled Himself by becoming obedient to the point of death," not just any death, but "death on a cross." Therefore, God exalted Him to the highest place (see Phil. 2:7-9). Jesus is the prime example that the way to exalted living, life's highest level, is through the door of humility.

Point blank the question was asked: "What does the Lord require of you?" The prophet answered, "To do justice, to love kindness, and to walk humbly with your God" (Mic. 6:8). The Bible declares that God does not seek first our outward sacrifices but a humble spirit (Ps. 51:17). Jesus said that the ones who humble themselves are the ones who will be exalted.

In an x-ray waiting room of a Kansas hospital hangs a framed quote from Shakespeare. It is from *Hamlet,* act 3, scene 4, the scene in which Hamlet produces a play making his parents appear guilty of murder. Hamlet pushes his mother, Gertrude, into a chair and says, "Come, come. Sit you down. You budge not. You go not hence while I set up a glass that you might see the inmost part of you." Pretty appropriate for an x-ray waiting room, is it not? Having humility involves coming before God and letting Him show us our inmost part.

What does being humble mean? What is humility? Isaiah 6 shows us it is to admit our sinfulness before God. Deuteronomy 8 declares it is to pledge our obedience to God. First Kings 22 (Micaiah) asserts it is submission to God. All of Scripture tells us humility is the first step to all of God's loving goodness.

Humility and Salvation

Humility is the first step to salvation and peace with God. The Word asserts God resists the proud but gives grace to the humble (Jas. 4:6; 1 Pet. 5:5).

Have you wondered why people do not stand in line to learn how to come to Jesus? Almost everyone knows we all will die if Jesus doesn't return first. Most folks are pretty sure we will be judged by God. Many people know that Jesus

Christ wants to give us eternal life. Why do they not take it? How can they put it off? Why do they wait?

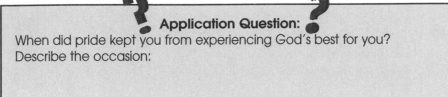

Application Question:
When did pride kept you from experiencing God's best for you?
Describe the occasion:

Pride keeps people from humbling themselves. Pride says, *You do not need to admit your sinfulness to God or anyone else.* Pride sneers, *You do not want to obey God. You are doing your own thing.* Pride puffs, *Submission to God? Not me.*

In the Beatitudes, Jesus described the blessed, the spiritually prosperous and happy people of the world. The Beatitudes are not statements haphazardly thrown together like a tossed salad of God's goodies. They show progression. The first Beatitude is the foundation for all the others—the beginning place for eternal prosperity and peace. "Blessed are the poor in spirit, for theirs is the kingdom of heaven" (Matt. 5:3). The admission of our sinfulness, the acknowledgment of our poverty of spirit, is the unavoidable first step toward the kingdom of heaven. You cannot have the kingdom of heaven when you think you are king.

Humility and Restoration

Humility also is the secret of restoring the joy of salvation. When you discover that you are no longer walking with the Lord and have wandered into a putrid swamp of self-centered living, humility is the way back to Him.

The people in the church in Ephesus were religiously active. They worked hard. They did not quit. They would not give in to the wickedness around them. Jesus told them, however, they were in danger of losing the right to represent Him because they had strayed from their earlier love for Him. In the beginning of their relationship with Him, they had humbly acknowledged their sins, repented of them, and followed Him. Perhaps they had become experts at pointing out other people's sins and had become blind to their own (Rev. 2:1-7).

God told Solomon when the temple was dedicated that the building was fine. God liked it, but He was more concerned about the hearts and souls of His people. God said that when the people would become proud and arrogant and would have to be punished, "If . . . My people who are called by My name humble themselves and pray, and seek My face and turn from their wicked ways, then

I will hear from heaven, will forgive their sin, and will heal their land" (2 Chron. 7:14).

Humility and Confident Living

Humility is the first step to salvation and the ongoing way to live in joyful fellowship with God. Humility is thus the secret of confident living, of godly self-esteem. One of the wrong concepts of humility is that it signifies being a wimp. Rather, it is about recognizing that the source of our strength is not in ourselves. Humility means putting confidence in the love, mercy, and strength of God. Doing that frees us to live confidently.

The clues for confident living are scattered all over the pages of God's Word. Near the end of Paul's life in the last of the New Testament writings, he expressed his confidence to Timothy, "I know whom I have believed and I am convinced that He is able to guard what I have entrusted to Him until that day" (2 Tim. 1:12). "That day" refers to the day of his going to be with God.

"He is able" is the recurring phrase of confidence. He is "able to keep you from stumbling" (Jude 24). He "is able to do exceeding abundantly beyond all that we ask or think" (Eph. 3:20). "Blessed be the God and Father of our Lord Jesus Christ, who according to His great mercy has caused us to be born again to a living hope through the resurrection of Jesus Christ from the dead, to obtain an inheritance which is imperishable and undefiled and will not fade away, reserved in heaven for you, who are protected by the power of God" (1 Pet. 1:3-5).

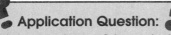

Application Question:
How do you demonstrate confidence in Jesus?

Have you ever wondered why God insists that we humble ourselves to let Him be number one in our lives? If He loves us, why not let us be number one? Is God on some kind of ego kick? Is He vain? No; He knows the truth about us. You and I tend to feel about ourselves what we think the most important person in our life feels about us. You may have an extremely high IQ, but if you think the most important person in your life thinks you are dumb, you will feel and act dumb. You may be the most handsome and most beautiful around; but if you think the most important person in your life thinks you are ugly, you will feel and act as if you are unattractive.

God in His love calls you to come humbly to Him and to make Him the most important Person in your life. As you do that, you will know you are loved because the most important Person in your life loves you and He died for you. You will have that godly self-esteem, rooted in God's esteem for you. You will live confidently in the security of His power, the grace of His cleansing, and the warmth of His love.

Humility and Successful Living

Humility is the first step to salvation and to spiritual restoration. Humility is the secret of confident living. Also, humility results in successful living. *Humble yourself and you will be exalted,* promises our Lord. Proverbs 11:2 declares, "When pride comes, then comes dishonor, but with the humble is wisdom." Humility brings honor. "The fear of the Lord is the instruction for wisdom, and before honor comes humility" (Prov. 15:33).

In a sense, humility is your greatest act. Jesus said, "Everyone who exalts himself shall be humbled, and he who humbles himself shall be exalted." Do you see it? *Everyone* will be humbled. Even the proudest egomaniac on earth will be humbled. The question of life's success is not Will I become humble? Yes, you will. We all will. The question is Will I humble myself, or will life or the Lord have to humble me? You will be humbled. If He does it, you will face punishment and failure. If you do it, you will have reward and success.

One word of caution: God Himself exalts us; He pronounces our lives successful. A successful life in God's eyes is one that humbly fulfills His purposes for that life. This may or may not have any relation to what the world calls success. Jesus lived the most successful life ever lived and was exalted above all others in creation (Phil. 2:9). Yet in His earthly life He owned no real estate, no business, no earthly investments. Let God, not the world, define successful living.

Humility is the way to the highest level of living. Are you willing now to say, *Oh, Lord, I humble myself before you. I admit my sinfulness. I trust You to forgive me. I pledge my obedience to you. I offer my submission.* In doing that, you begin your walk toward exalted living.

YOUR NOTES

(LUKE 18:9-14)

Humility and Pride (Luke 18:9-14)

The parable about the chief seats shows that we are to base our self-esteem on the humble acceptance of God's love, not the self-centered evaluation of this world. The parable about the Pharisee and the tax-gatherer reveals how easily we evaluate other people by superficial, worldly standards.

One of my favorite memories of growing up as a country kid in a rural area was going to town. Usually our family did this on Saturday. My dad would give me 25 cents and solemnly say, "Son, do not spend it all in one place;" and I did not. At the drug store I bought a cherry coke for 5 cents. I also bought a candy bar for another nickel. I went to the movie for 8 cents. I don't remember what happened to the other 7 cents, but I'm pretty sure it didn't go into my retirement fund.

The best buy was the movie! We saw cartoons and serials—those short stories continued from week to week so you would come back. The western movies were the best part of all. Each western had the good guys and the bad guys; and you could tell them apart; and the story would always come out right. The good guys wore white hats, never got dirty, and spoke good language. The bad guys wore dark hats and clothes. They did not have good vocabularies. They were always dirty. In the middle of the story, after a fight or some other exciting thing, the good guys like Roy Rogers and Gene Autry would play their guitars and sing a little song for us.

I remember going to Vacation Bible School and hearing for the first time the stories about David, and I thought David must look like Roy Rogers or Gene Autry. He could fight and he could then get out his harp and play a song. I was sure David wore a white hat.

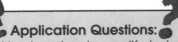

Application Questions:
Are good and bad as clear in your life today as they used to be? How/how not?

Additional Confusion

In Jesus' parable about the Pharisee and the tax-gatherer, we may become a bit confused as to who is the good guy and who is the bad guy. We have been conditioned to think of the Pharisees as the bad guys. We know this tax-gatherer was not a good guy, for he admitted that; but he was good in that he realized he was bad.

This story was terribly confusing to the people who first heard it. They saw the Pharisees as highly respected men in their community, sincerely religious men. Pharisees as a group were trying to obey Psalm 1 and "not walk in the counsel of the wicked, nor stand in the path of sinners, nor sit in the seat of scoffers!" They were committed to living a separated life for God.

When the Pharisee prayed and said, "I am not like other people: swindlers, unjust, adulterers, or even like this tax-gatherer," he was telling the truth. He was not like many people in his sinful, dishonest, and adulterous society. He said, "I fast twice a week." Most religious people fasted once a week in Jesus' day. The Levitical law required only that they fast once a year, on the Day of Atonement. This man fasted every Monday and every Thursday.

Learning Activity 2
PHARISEES AND TAX-GATHERERS
Use this space to take notes:

A First-Century View of . . .
     A Pharisee   A Tax-gatherer

A Twentieth-Century View of . . .
     A Pharisee   A Tax-gatherer

The Pharisee also said, "I pay tithes of all I get." Most religious folk gave a tithe, but he implied, *I make sure that I pay a tithe on every bit of gain, exempting nothing. I am willing to have a lower standard of living in order to pay my tithes.* He was telling the truth!

Well, what about the tax-gatherer in Jesus' story? He looks OK. He seems to be a good-natured fellow who knows his faults and accepts his limitations. In that day, however, people

"Two men went . . . to pray."

generally hated tax-gatherers. Jesus was criticized numerous times for being in their company.

To understand the hostility toward the tax-gatherers, we need to understand how one became a tax-gatherer and what the tax-gatherers did. Rome sold to the highest bidder the right to collect taxes. The one granted the position of tax-gatherer would pay to Rome the amount he bid, and anything over that amount he kept. He could collect from the people all he could get—absolutely no limit. He could demand all the traffic allowed, and he had the power of the Roman military to back him up. A merchant selling goods in the city had to pay a tax for the privilege. If he transported goods from one place to another, the merchant had to go by the office of the tax-gatherer both coming and going. Extortion was a common and accepted practice among those in this profession. Injustice was just a way of life. In fact, a Roman historian told of one city having an honest tax-gatherer. This was so unusual and exciting to them that they erected a statue of him in the town square.

If both of these men—the tax-gatherer and the Pharisee—were running for office, all of us would have voted for the Pharisee. If both of them were courting your sister, you would want her to marry the Pharisee.

Arrogant Conceit

What made the one who would have been unanimously proclaimed as the good guy, the bad guy? What were these two doing that made one good and the other bad? Both had gone to church; both were praying. Going to church and praying are good, right? Not until we read the Pharisee's prayer do we begin to get a hint of what made him one of the bad guys. He was conceited. He was telling the truth, yes; but he was conceited. We do not like conceit, do we? Dizzy Dean used to say, "If you done it, it ain't bragging"; but it is.

I like to play golf. I do not play often, usually twice a month. I never practice, so naturally I am not very good. Probably if I played more and practiced a lot, I still would not be very good. One day I was playing my usual game with a friend who is rather conceited. He can strut sitting down. On one attempt I experienced one of those rare moments when the golf club and the ball were in the same place at that perfect time, and I hit the shot of a lifetime for me. My friend said, "Great shot, Frank! Right down there by mine!" Well, what he said was true; but it was not good.

The Pharisee said, *I thank you that I am not like other people. I do all these things that are good.* He was telling the truth, but it was conceit. His heart was completely empty of humility.

A radio preacher, after delivering a sermon called "Maturity in the Spirit," asked his listeners to send in letters about their Christian lives. One man wrote, "I am glad to write you about my Christian life. I do not smoke; I do not touch alcohol; I do not gamble; I am faithful to my wife and never look at another woman; I work hard; I never go to the movies; I go to bed early every night; I rise with the dawn. I have been living like this for three years now, but just wait till next spring when they let me out of this place!"

The Pharisee was not in prison. He did not have to live as he did. He had chosen to live the good life; but he was conceited, and behind the man's conceit was pride. Pride is a most serious sin to God. "Pride and arrogance . . . I hate," said God (Prov. 8:13). "When pride comes, then comes dishonor." (Prov. 11:2). "Pride goes before destruction" (Prov. 16:18). "A man's pride will bring him low" (Prov. 29:23). "Love does not brag and is not arrogant (1 Cor. 13:4). "God is opposed to the proud, but gives grace to the humble" (Jas. 4:6). Spiritual pride is religion turned rancid.

Like many of us, the Pharisee had many advantages. He had been born in a family within a nation where loving God was taught as a way of life. He had learned about the grace of God and the truth of God. He had the privilege of an education most people did not have. He began to say to himself, *I am special. I have the truth. I live the good life. God loves me more than most people.* He began to be confident in his own righteousness and to look down on everybody else.

Church folk can become sinfully proud. Having been blessed by the grace of God, having received the truth of God, we can find ourselves thinking, *Look at us. We are special. We are better and closer to God than the others.* We can begin to look down on others. Students and faculty of Christian colleges and seminaries can be infected with this pride, believing in their own righteousness while looking down on everybody else. Pride has the nauseating stench of self-centeredness.

We are wise continually to examine our hearts for evidences of spiritual pride. All of us are susceptible to pride's subtle approach. For instance, in a Sunday School class a dear teacher told her young students, "Let us bow our heads and thank God we are not like that terrible Pharisee."

Admirable Confession

The tax-gatherer could have prayed, *I thank you, God, that I am not like the Pharisee. I did not come in here acting high and mighty. I am not perfect, but at least I am no hypocrite.* The thing that most galvanizes my gallbladder is the idea that hypocrisy is the only sin. Some say, "Well, I know I do wrong things; but at least I do not try to hide them." Then they lay their dirty laundry out for all to see as though it is all right as long as they don't hide it.

In Dallas two men robbed a bank. One of them, for some reason, did not wear a mask. The other one did. In 15 minutes they were caught. Can you imagine that bank robber going before a judge and saying, "Yes, your Honor, I did it; but I didn't try to cover it up. I didn't wear a mask." Should he

YOUR NOTES

(LUKE 18:9-14)

125

reasonably expect to be let off simply because he did not try to hide his wrong?

What happens to people who are confident in their own righteousness and look down on everybody else? Jesus told this simple story of a good guy whose pride had corrupted his heart and a bad guy whose corrupt heart was made righteous in God's sight. The good guy thanked God for how good he himself was; the bad guy came humbly before God to confess his sins and to seek forgiveness. The tax-gatherer was forgiven and declared just in God's sight; the Pharisee was not. To make sure you and I would not miss the point, Jesus said, "everyone who exalts himself shall be humbled, but he who humbles himself shall be exalted" (18:14).

So what do we do? We stand in the presence of God and look to Him. People who are self-centered and spiritually proud look at themselves, look at others, but seldom look to God. When we come into God's presence, we actually begin to see ourselves as we are. When we see ourselves, we will see our sin. When we see our sin, we will see our need to repent.

Isaiah went to church and had a vision of God. There this dedicated religious man saw himself and said, "Woe is me, . . . I am a man of unclean lips" (Isa. 6:5).

Paul wrote his last two letters to Timothy. In the first letter he said, "It is a trustworthy statement, deserving full acceptance, that Christ Jesus came into the world to save sinners, among whom I am foremost of all" (1 Tim. 1:15). Notice the verb tense: not I *was* the foremost or worst of sinners, but I *am* the worst. Paul had left everything this world thinks important to follow Jesus. How could he say that? Because he was not looking at himself and others, comparing himself with them. He was looking at himself and God; for his next words were, "Now to the King eternal, immortal, invisible, the only God, be honor and glory for ever and ever. Amen" (1 Tim. 1:17).

At a meeting in a Southern Baptist seminary, Billy Graham was answering questions posed by the students. One student said, "Dr. Graham, I have noticed that you are a humble man. You are in a position to assert a great deal more authority than you do. Is this humility a trait of your family?" I was there and this is how I remember his answer, "Young man, I have had a lot of experiences that could make me proud, but God commands us to be humble. Humility is not something some people are and some are not. It is a command of God."

The Bible commands, "All of you, clothe yourselves with humility toward one another, for God is opposed to the proud, but gives grace to the humble. Humble yourselves, therefore, under the mighty hand of God, that He may exalt you at the proper time" (1 Pet. 5:5-6). "Whoever exalts himself shall be humbled; and whoever humbles himself shall be exalted" (Matt. 23:12).

CHRISTIAN GROWTH STUDY PLAN

Preparing Christians to Serve

In the **Christian Growth Study Plan (formerly Church Study Course)**, this book *Timely Answers to Key Questions (A Study of Selected Parables Unique to the Gospel of Luke)* is a resource for credit in the course Developing Teaching Skills of the Reaching People Through Bible Study Projects and Groups Diploma Plan and in the subject area Biblical Studies in the Christian Growth category of diploma plans. To receive credit, read the book, complete the learning activities, show your work to your pastor, a staff member or church leader, then complete the information on the next page. The form may be duplicated. Send the completed page to:

Christian Growth Study Plan
127 Ninth Avenue, North, MSN 117
Nashville, TN 37234-0117
FAX: (615) 251-5067

For information about the Christian Growth Study Plan, refer to the current Christian Growth Study Plan Catalog. Your church office may have a copy. If not, request a free copy from the Christian Growth Study Plan office (615/251-2525).

Course Credit Information

Please check the appropriate boxes indicating the course(s) for which you want to receive credit.

☐ Developing Teaching Skills (LS-0053)   ☐ Biblical Studies (CG-0374)

PARTICIPANT INFORMATION

Social Security Number	Personal CGSP Number*	Date of Birth
_ _ _ - _ _ - _ _ _ _	_ _ _ - _ _ - _ _ _ _	_ _ - _ _ - _ _

Name (First, MI, Last)

☐ Mr.   ☐ Miss
☐ Mrs. ☐

| Address (Street, Route, or P.O. Box) | City, State | Home Phone _ _ _ - _ _ _ - _ _ _ _ | Zip Code |

CHURCH INFORMATION

Church Name

| Address (Street, Route, or P.O. Box) | City, State | Zip Code |

CHANGE REQUEST ONLY

☐ Former Name

| ☐ Former Address | City, State | Zip Code |

| ☐ Former Church | City, State | Zip Code |

| Signature of Pastor, Conference Leader, or Other Church Leader | Date |

*New participants are requested but not required to give SS# and date of birth. Existing participants, please give CGSP# when using SS# for the first time. Thereafter, only one ID# is required. *Mail To:* Christian Growth Study Plan, 127 Ninth Ave., North, MSN 117, Nashville, TN 37234-0117. Fax: (615)251-5067